GOLIATH SLAYERS

Many times we are straining so hard to see the big blessings that we miss the abundance of small ones along the way.

Never underestimate the power of God's Word.

ISBN- 13-978-19834-80461
ISBN-10-198-348-0460
Library of Congress: TX 8-605-689
Effective Date of Registration June 24, 2018

GOLIATH SLAYERS

A Handbook for Prayer Warriors

Things may seem like they're getting worse before they get better... but eventually they will get better as He will not give us something worse than we asked for. Job's situation worsened before it got better and he was blessed far more in the end than the beginning. He was declared righteous by the Lord God, yet calamity struck him numerous times. Christians are not immune to life's challenges simply because they are the righteous Children of God. There hath no temptation taken you but such as is common to man: but God is faithful, who will not suffer you to be tempted above that ye are able; but will with the temptation also make a way to escape, that ye may be able to bear it. 1 Cor.10:13

Contents

Dedication

All honor and glory are due to my Lord and Savior Jesus Christ for His unswerving love, wisdom, patience, and compassion in allowing me the privilege of writing this treatise.

+

Effectual prayer goes far beyond the childhood prayers such as "Now I lay me down to sleep, if I should die before I wake, I pray the Lord my soul to take" or "God is good, God is great . . . ". They served their purpose while we were children, however, we must learn to put away childish things" 1 Cor. 13:11.

9 Or what man is there of you, whom if his son ask bread, will he give him a stone?
10 Or if he ask a fish, will he give him a serpent?
Will God give us the opposite of what we ask for? Matt. 7:9-10.

Introduction

How ironic!

Here I am writing a book on prayer, intended firstly for myself, pining away in my own personal misery and the Lord has to remind me to pray, not once or twice but three times! I mean, how absurd! How rrogant, that while smugly editing my own works, I should neglect to pray for the giants in my own personal life! Is there a message here?

Goliath symbolizes the giants natural or spiritual we face every day in our lives. Giants like David faced are bigger than ourselves or whatever mankind is unable to conquer. Giants of financial, relational, home grown, recurring sins, emotional, mental, sickness, disease, abuse of all sorts, including substance abuse, loss through the death of a loved one, self esteem or self image, divorce, unemployment, prodigal children, toxic people in our lives the list is endless. Unfortunately, many of God's people are cowering in the trenches not knowing how or what to o against the giants they are facing. Plus, to further complicate things, many are facing multiple giants simultaneously…even over a prolonged period of time. Furthermore, every soldier has the potential of being wounded in battle, hence the need to trained Prayer Warriors to back you up. Just because you're saved doesn't mean you're ready to intercede on behalf of another.
Which reminds me of why I like war movies so much: men and women enlist into the service of their choice be it Army, Navy, Air Force, Marines or Coast Guard. First they go through a mandatory Boot Camp or Basic Training to familiarize themselves with military

life and jargon. From there it's off to a more precise training such as the motor pool, aircraft maintenance, even fire fighting, military police or communications. There is a host of other necessary jobs one can be trained to perform. Some even go to OCS, Officer Candidate School/Academy, to learn leadership and battle strategies.

The point is such training is typical of what the church needs to be doing, *perfecting the saints for the work of the ministry, for the edifying of the body f Christ* Eph.4:12b.

Both natural and spiritual

So far we've covered giants in the natural realm, but what about the spiritual realm? Certainly many of the giants facing Jesus and the disciples were in fact instigated by demonic or *the wiles of the devil rulers of darkness and spiritual wickedness in high places* Ephesians 6:11-12. We must remember that *the thief cometh not, but to steal, kill, and to destroy* John 10:10a. This covers both the natural and spiritual for the natural is instigated by the spiritual. Numerous times I've witnessed "prayer warriors" attempt to exorcise a demon without first discerning, but presuming that all sickness and disease is caused by demonic possession and not oppression. Disastrous!

We must remember that David faced both a spiritual and natural giant, one who opposed Israel from a natural enemy but also spiritual as Israel was the Philistine's enemy on the spiritual front just as he is today. So often we pray for the natural and forget the spirit realm. It's a delicate matter to say the least. One must be aware of both realms and be prepared for both. If it were merely a matter of the flesh, perhaps Jesus would not have had the need to shed

His blood. As we ponder the prayers of Jesus and the apostles we clearly see both realms. That's why as Prayer Warriors we need to be trained in both realms.

1Samuel 17:1-58 chronicles the account of David slaying the Philistine giant, Goliath, while the armies of Israel, under King Saul, cowered in trenches awaiting Israel's champion, a young shepherd boy named David, to defeat oliath's challenge. David had already slain a bear and a lion by God's hand and he was not afraid to face the uncircumcised Philistine giant.

Remember, David would not use the conventional armor of the day, so he put it off in favor of that which he'd already tested and found true…the name of the Lord. That is what we, as *Goliath Slayers* must learn to do. David knew how to use a sling…and he defeated the giant with one simple smooth stone, in the name of the Lord.

Note: Every Prayer Warrior must remember that unless they are trained in counseling, either secular or Christian, you simply are not qualified to pursue in-depth counseling. There is a point a person needs to be referred to professionals. Only ask questions pertinent to praying appropriately. Secular counselors normally referring to the natural realm and Christian counseling is usually attributed to the spiritual realm. Remember, David refused to use the armor given him by King Saul in favor of that which he'd already proven and in actuality David would be classified in the spiritual realm because he came in the name of the Lord.

Make certain Goliath is dead

It wasn't enough for Goliath to lay fallen at his feet, David had to cut off his head and display it openly 1Samuel 17. The display of his head was a time of joy and praise for the children of Israel. So also whenever we have a victory, no matter how big or small, we ought to share it with others, especially those who have labored with us in prayer. Our giants of the past have a way of haunting us in the future. Remember, God has forgiven us but did not give us a spirit of amnesia. A giant is not dead if we harbor resentment and unforgiveness.

Recently archeologists have reported, though unsubstantiated, discovering the skeletal remains of Goliath, however if the head is still attached it isn't Goliath. It may be one of his brothers.

Sons of Anak

Anak's sons are named in Numbers 13:22-33 as Ahiman, Sheshai, and Talmai, whether or not they are the brothers of Goliath may be debated, however it is widely assumed they are brothers of Goliath…all giants, Goliath being 9 feet tall it's safe o say his brothers were also huge and as brothers it's also safe to assume they would fight for one another, thus possibly explaining David's selection of four or five stones in case he had to fight them as well. However, I find it curious that the other brothers are not mentioned in the text.

Our armor and weapons

I have never heard of an army not being skillfully trained on its weapons---yet the Christian church, the greatest army ever assembled, is mostly untrained saved for the few who have taken the time to be properly trained. Tragically even many of those in position of leadership are either poorly trained or not at all. No wonder the church is having such a difficult time and sometimes running scared much like King Saul's army when they faced Goliath. The pastors cannot handle it all they must train the general assembly *for the work of the ministry, for the edifying of the body of Christ.* Eph. 4:12b

Ephesians 6:10-18 lists the armor and weapons in which we are to put on and use daily. Without it we are doomed to failure and destruction---and Satan knows it! This passage confronts both the natural and spiritual realms.

> 10-11. We are to put on all the armour of God. And stand strong in the Lord and the power of His might. [Not our flesh].

> > 13 Our enemies are spiritual, not flesh and blood, but principalities and powers and rulers of darkness [not necessarily demonic possession]. John 10:10 refers to evil or Satanic attack primarily as a natural attack without necessarily being possessed by demons. Likewise Job's wrestling though his battles were chronicled as Satanic attacks in the natural, nevertheless were also spiritual as no mention of demonic possession is mentioned.

13. We are to put on <u>all</u> the armour to stand. Not just a part of it.
14. We stand in truth and righteousness. Not lies and deceit.
15. Prepared with the gospel of peace. [Peace with God].
16. Faith is our shield to quench the fiery onslaught of the wicked.
17. Salvation protects our mind.
18. We are to pray always with supplication [humble petition]. Watching with all perseverance for all saints.

Prayer is warfare! No matter if you're praying for yourself or another---prayer is warring against the forces of evil [spiritual] Ephesians 6:10-19 and we must be prepared for the fight to the very end! Frustration sets in for either of two reasons or both:

1. The Christian church, in general, has not been properly trained for spiritual warfare. As the result we have become an army untrained in the use of out armory Ephesians 4:12.
2. We are fighting spiritual battles on our own, in the flesh, instead of the Spirit.

Prayer, at times, can be overwhelming with all the requests, personal, family, loved ones, sickness, relationships, government the list goes on and on especially when they seemingly inundate you all at one time without giving one time for a short breath. Don't let it be a coffee break!

Only the Spirit can fight spiritual battles. We often quote passages like these without a clue as to their relevance to our lives.

[3]*For though we walk in the flesh, we do not war after the flesh:* I often wonder if we're fighting spiritual battles in the flesh. I know I've been guilty of fighting in the flesh from time to time.

[4] *(For the weapons of our warfare are not carnal, but mighty through God to the pulling down of strongholds ;)* there is a spiritual battle without demonic possession.

[5] *Casting down imaginations and every high thing that exalteth itself against the knowledge of God, and bringing into captivity every thought to the obedience of Christ;*

[6] *And having in a readiness to revenge all disobedience, when your obedience is fulfilled.*

I wonder how often we forget this vital principal and wage war in the flesh?

[10] *Finally, my brethren, be strong in the Lord, and in the power of his might.*

[11] *Put on the whole armour of God that ye may be able to stand against the wiles of the devil.*

[12] *For we wrestle not against flesh and blood, but against principalities, against powers, against the rulers of the darkness of this world, against spiritual wickedness in high places.*

[13] *Wherefore take unto you the whole armour of God, that ye may be able to withstand in the evil day, and having done*

all, to stand. Quite simply many are falling simply because they have not put on the *whole armour of God.* They have not been properly equipped and trained.

[14] *Stand therefore, having your loins girt about with truth, and having on the breastplate of righteousness;*

[15] *And your feet shod with the preparation of the gospel of peace;*

[16] *Above all, taking the shield of faith, wherewith ye shall be able to quench all the fiery darts of the wicked.*

[17] *And take the helmet of salvation, and the sword of the Spirit, which is the word of God:*

[18] *Praying always with all prayer and supplication in the Spirit, and watching thereunto with all perseverance and supplication for all saints;*

[19] *And for me, that utterance may be given unto me, that I may open my mouth boldly, to make known the mystery of the gospel,* Eph.6:10-19. Without this passage we are defeated in warfare fighting in our own power our armory depleted.

From time to time we are called upon to intercede on behalf of another thus we have become *Goliath Slayers,* be it through one on one or on a prayer team or even for ourselves personally. It must not be taken lightly. The term "Prayer Warrior", though not found in Scripture, is none the less a reality. "Warrior" is a term used of soldiers in battle. Likewise "Prayer

Warriors" often find themselves on the front lines, in the trenches, so to speak, praying for or interceding for another. Hence, to join an after service prayer team is no small task and must be considered diligently, even to do hospital or home visitation is a serious undertaking. Prayer is warfare!

It is therefore vital that one understands the potential for "getting over one's head". Prolonged prayerful intercession with another's giants and issues can wear on you after a time, especially when you don't comprehend you are fighting both the natural and spiritual. I have found that a person requesting prayer quite often will first ask for a generic prayer, to which a few well directed questions will lead to a more direct request, which may often lead to more questions revealing more issues than originally thought. The more questions, the more issues or giants, in the natural, to be concerned with, hence the idea of a Prayer Warrior. Add the spiritual aspect and it further complicates things unless you're fully prepared.

Most certainly the Church is mandated by Scripture to intercede on behalf of one another, *Bear ye one another's burdens, and so fulfil the law of Christ* Gal.6:2 comes to mind as it is in direct reference to the Altar of Incense of which we are about to study. Indeed to be called upon to pray or intercede for another is a great privilege and honor as all of us have issues beyond our finite beings that we aren't equipped to handle on our own. The thought that simply because you are a Christian automatically qualifies you to pray or intercede on behalf or another is not always grounds for you to proceed.

It is for this cause I have included the Old Testament roots of prayer in particular the Altar of Incense and the fragrant spices used to create the sweet smelling savor acceptable to God as only specific spices were acceptable for prayers to be answered. So also today many of our prayers are not answered because we use the wrong ingredients. To understand the Old Testament Altar of Incense is to understand the New Testament prayers.

Writing about prayer is relatively easy, putting it into practice…not so easy. Perhaps the biggest obstacle is the flesh, the old sin nature. Prayer, too, needs to be reborn as does hearing God's voice. All too often I've acted on what I "thought" was God's voice only to learn later, and after consuming a full pie of humility, that it was not God's voice but my flesh, my old sin nature, acting from emotions pride or adrenalin. When it's God speaking and directing, it comes to pass exactly as spoken. But the flesh is fickle, given to change and chance leading to frustration, humiliation and error.

Just as it is important to speak and pray God's Word over a person, it is doubly vital to speak exactly which passage to speak. We can memorize a ton of Scripture, but totally miss it if we don't have exactly what the Father wants for that person at the exact time. For example, if a person is having a financial crisis it's of no use to quote a verse on end times. That's why I emphasize learning to hear His voice at all times for therein will power be made manifest.

Jesus always did and said as the Father directed, therefore accomplishing exactly what the Father directed. He is our pattern and we must emulate Him.

Battle fatigue

Waging war in the natural obviously produces battle fatigue; so also spiritual warfare may produce battle weary soldiers, especially those in fulltime ministry. I firmly believe we *are to fight the good fight of faith* 1Timothy 6:12. Fatigue comes when we're fighting in our own strength instead of relying on the Lord. *Hast thou not known? Hast thou not heard, that the everlasting God, the Lord, the creator of the ends of the earth, fainth not, neither is weary? There is no searching of His understanding.* [29] *He giveth power to the faint; and to them that have no might He increaseth strength.* [30] *Even the youths shall faint and be weary, and the young men shall utterly fall:* [31] *But they that wait upon the Lord shall renew their strength; they shall run and not be weary; and they shall walk, and not faint.* Isa.40:28-31.

Little did I know when I began writing this book that I'd literally experience every emotion described herein while seeking healing from Parkinson's Disease; Psalm 66:16-20 has become my peace in troublesome times.

The intent of this treatise is not to endorse or discredit practices by any denomination or individual. Its sole intent is to present the Biblical view.

It matters not the cause or severity of the sickness or disease and it matters not what the disease or sickness is. . . nothing is beyond the healing power of God's Word

Chapter 1

Prayer and the Old Testament pattern

To be an effective Prayer Warrior one must have an understanding of the Old Testament Altar of Incense and how it works. Without an understanding one is destined to failure and frustration. Unfortunately prayer is much understood even by some who stand as intercessors as well as those petitioning on their own behalf. I personally find it unwise and inadvisable to allow one to be on an after service prayer line to intercede without proper training. It is therefore my intent to bring an understanding and clarity to all seeking the Lord for their own needs or of others.

To understand prayer we must first realize:

- Prayer is a gift from God and no other religion has the capacity to communicate with their god.
- Prayer is therefore a HOLY communication between ourselves and our Heavenly Father.
- Prayer is also a gift from one person to another as no other religion has the capacity to intercede on behalf of another.

To study the Old Testament Altar of Incense does not mean we are to build a physical altar with all its ingredients verbatim as recorded in Exodus 30:1-9, rather it is meant to a pattern that foreshadows the prayers of the New Testament. Likewise Jesus, in answer to the disciples request for learning to pray, was in fact a model or pattern for prayer not intended for recitation Luke 11:1-13. It may well that Jesus' instructions to His disciples were the New Testament variation of the Old Testament Altar of Incense [note the absence of animosity and negative attitudes]. Also He was not creating a new pattern for prayer, destroying the old, but simply building on Moses' Altar of Incense. Nor was Jesus establishing a "new phenomena". Remember, every New Testament teaching has its roots in the Old Testament including prayer.

[1] *And it came to pass, that, as he was praying in* **a** *certain place, when he ceased, one of his disciples said unto him, Lord, teach us to pray, as John also taught his disciples.* This is Jesus' pattern for the disciples to pray. It is sometimes erroneously called "the sinner's prayer" but Jesus never prayed this prayer as he was sinless. He used it as a pattern, not to merely be recited, as many are taught to do. I wonder if Jesus' pattern wasn't the same as the Altar of Incense Moses had built for the Tabernacle in the Wilderness.

[2] *And he said unto them, When ye pray, say, Our Father which art in heaven, Hallowed be thy name. Thy kingdom come. Thy will be done, as in heaven, so in earth.* "Our Father which art in heaven" automatically gives acclaim of our relationship to God. He is our Heavenly Father. It is adoration for our Heavenly Father. Thus prayer is to begin with adoration and exultation of our Heavenly Father and it's inclusive of the Father's will being accomplished as opposed to our own will.

[3] *Give us day by day our daily bread.* Not only food for the body but also for the soul and spirit. It recognizes the Living God as our provider, that without Him we are indeed insufficient.

[4] *And forgive us our sins; for we also forgive every one that is indebted to us. And lead us not into temptation; but deliver us from evil.* Forgiveness is required for answered prayer. It is also necessary to pray for protection from temptation when we're tempted.

[5] *And he said unto them, Which of you shall have a friend, and shall go unto him at midnight, and say unto him, Friend, lend me three loaves;* (Admonishing humility, servitude and love toward one another) also proclaiming our friendship with the Father and not enemies.

[6] *For a friend of mine in his journey is come to me, and I have nothing to set before him?* This speaks of sympathy and concern leading to the compassion of actually helping instead of mere pity.

[7] *And he from within shall answer and say, Trouble me not: the door is now shut, and my children are with me in bed; I cannot rise and give thee.*

[8] *I say unto you, Though he will not rise and give him, because he is his friend, yet because of his importunity he will rise and give him as many as he needeth.* Compassion is now administered, after the need is acknowledged.

[9]And *I say unto you, Ask, and it shall be given you; seek, and ye shall find; knock, and it shall be opened unto you.* Persistence! Holding on to the horns of the Altar of Incense represents persistence…not pride or arrogance.

10 *For every one that asketh receiveth; and he that seeketh findeth; and to him that knocketh it shall be opened.* Persistence [horns of the altar]! Our prayers are answered in God's timing, not ours. See Divine Delays. Many give up before the victory is realized.

11 *If a son shall ask bread of any of you that is a father, will he give him a stone? Or if he ask a fish, will he for a fish give him a serpent?* God's integrity!

12 *Or if he shall ask an egg, will he offer him a scorpion?* God's integrity! [When the proper incense ingredients is manifest God will answer accordingly]

13 If *ye then, being evil, know how to give good gifts unto your children: how much more shall your*

Virtually every Old Testament book is replete with prayers. Prayers of praise, worship, divine help, mercy, wisdom, grace, literally every subject a man could need.

- They prayed deliberately, with persistence and passion from the heart.
- They prayed for themselves, kings, relatives, the lost, and kingdoms.
- They all prayed to the God of heaven and earth, Jehovah the Creator.
- They prayed at all hours of the day and night.
- They asked for what they needed and wanted.
- They prayed humbly without arrogance or pride.

Altar of Incense

The Altar of Incense was a permanent fixture in the Old Testament Tabernacle and Solomon's Temple. Likewise it's a permanent fixture in the church today. It like the other pieces of furniture was only to be moved when the Tabernacle was moved as a whole. It was to be borne upon the shoulders of the priests and not to be placed on a cart to be drawn by oxen. This is a picture of the New Testament church, it is to bear the burdens or prayer requests upon their own shoulders. The Altar was located in the Holy Place and stood directly in front of the Veil which protected Ark of the Covenant in the Holy of Holies from the priests inadvertently entering. The Holy of Holies could only be entered once a year by the High Priest. Now Jesus, in effect, was informing the disciples that He was now the High Priest, that the Veil would be torn in two allowing everyone entrance to the Father. This made the Old Testament pattern void as a new and lasting pattern was established. Exodus 37:25; Leviticus 4:7-18.

The Altar of Incense had horns built onto the corners, which meant that you and I could take hold of those horns in persistence, not letting go until victory was attained.

- Fugitives could also take hold of the horns for mercy, thus symbolizing every sinner being allowed to approach God for mercy.

  - A fugitive might mean one who is running from a crime they've committed or an unbeliever seeking salvation.

- Abraham persisted in prayer for his nephew Lot and his family in Sodom Genesis 18:16-33.
- Read also Exodus 27:2; 1Kings 1:50-53; 12:26-30; Amos 3:14-15. Far too many hold off seeking help far too long either for spiritual or natural help. Many give up before the answer comes, thus we are admonished to hold on to the horns of the altar and not let go until victory

Altar of Incense and its construction

- Shittim wood overlaid with pure gold: the wood is a type of humanity covered with gold representing the Divine; the incarnation and deity of Christ. It also represents you and me as priests of the New Testament. Wood typifies humanity, overlaid with gold [typifying divinity or in our case righteousness], by the blood of Jesus, which represents our salvation. [There are about 1300 species of Acacia or Shittim wood, a hardwood, known for producing furniture, flooring and ornaments having an illustrious and durable finish.]
- Horns on the corners overlaid with gold: were primarily for fugitives to grab hold of to obtain mercy symbolizing remorse and conviction, persistence and not giving up; however the saints may grab hold

being persistent in prayer. Fugitives, for all practical purposes, are enemies of God, or those running for their lives from various crimes they've committed. Jesus made peace for us that we are now friends of God not enemies. As unbelievers we were once fugitives seeking God's mercy and forgiveness.

- Staves inserted in the golden rings, on the sides, were for the priests to carry the Altar on their shoulders when moved. <u>The staves were never to be removed</u>. As New Testament priests we are to carry one another's burdens/prayers Galatians 6:2. We are to be ready to offer prayer at any time or place and never stop praying.
- Incense was to be burned night and day with fire [this meaning that our prayers can be heard by the Lord God day or night 24/7. We need not wait until a special day or time to pray. Daniel prayed three times a day.

    a. Fire symbolizing fervent and intensity, as opposed to half heartedness.
    b. The incense itself was made of finely ground and crushed spices [speaks of Jesus' sufferings during the period of His opposition, trial, and crucifixion] mixed with :

        i. Salt: as a preservative and seasoning. Colossians 4:6; Matthew 5:13; Leviticus 2:13.

ii. Stacte: a fragrant gum from a tree. Deuteronomy 32:1-2.
iii. Onycha: ground shell fish from the Red Sea. Matthew 4:4.
iv. Galbanum: a gum from a plant or shrub. Used to ward off insects. Isaiah 53; Hebrews 5:7.
v. Frankincense: from the sap of a tree; purity and righteousness. Song of Solomon 4:6; John 19:39.

- The crushing represents a broken spirit and contrite heart to which God will not despise Ps.34:18; 51:17; Isa. 57:15; 66:2. Prayers will not and cannot be answered with a proud and haughty heart, James 4:6, 10; 1Peter 5:6.

These were the only five ingredients authorized to be used for the incense, anything else was and is contrary to God's directives and considered to be strange, vulgar and offensive incense, thus unacceptable. All of which means prayers full of lust, vengeance, anger, jealousy and such likeness are unacceptable. That's what is meant by no burnt sacrifice, nor meat, or drink offering was to be offered on the Altar of Incense. Ever hear someone say: "It feels like my prayers don't go higher than the ceiling"? Could it be that the wrong ingredients are mixed in the prayer incense thus causing unanswered prayers?

In addition to the spices Aaron made a blood atonement on the horns once a year which looked forward to Messiah shedding His blood on Calvary.

The following is the Old Testament pattern for prayer

Incense always represents prayer

1 *And thou shalt make an altar to burn incense upon: of shittim wood shalt thou make it.*

2 *A cubit shall be the length thereof, and a cubit the breadth thereof; foursquare shall it be: and two cubits shall be the height thereof: the horns thereof shall be of the same.*

3 *And thou shalt overlay it with pure gold, the top thereof, and the sides thereof round about, and the horns thereof; and thou shalt make unto it a crown of gold round about.*

4 *And two golden rings shalt thou make to it under the crown of it, by the two corners thereof, upon the two sides of it shalt thou make it; and they shall be for places for the staves to bear it withal.*

5 *And thou shalt make the staves of shittim wood, and overlay them with gold.*

6 *And thou shalt put it before the vail that is by the ark of the testimony, before the mercy seat that is over the testimony, where I will meet with thee.*

7 *And Aaron shall burn thereon sweet incense every morning: when he dresseth the lamps, he shall burn incense upon it.*

8 *And when Aaron lighteth the lamps at even, he shall burn incense upon it, a perpetual* [never ending] *incense before the Lord throughout your generations.*

9 *Ye shall offer no strange incense thereon, nor burnt sacrifice, nor meat offering; neither shall ye pour drink offering thereon.* No strange incense, today people are adding their own "spices and herbs" to God's ordained formula.

10 *And Aaron shall make an atonement upon the horns of it once in a year with the blood of the sin offering of atonements: once in the year shall he make atonement upon it throughout your generations: it is most holy unto the Lord.* Ex.30:1-10

1 *And it came to pass on the day that Moses had fully set up the tabernacle, and had anointed it, and sanctified it, and all the instruments thereof, both the altar and all the vessels thereof, and had anointed them, and sanctified them;*

2 *That the princes of Israel, heads of the house of their fathers, who were the princes of the tribes, and were over them that were numbered, offered:*

3 *And they brought their offering before the LORD, six covered wagons, and twelve oxen; a wagon for two of the princes, and for each one an ox: and they brought them before the tabernacle.*

4 *And the LORD spake unto Moses, saying,*

5 *Take it of them, that they may be to do the service of the tabernacle of the congregation; and thou shalt give them unto the Levites, to every man according to his service.*

6 *And Moses took the wagons and the oxen, and gave them unto the Levites.*

7 *Two wagons and four oxen he gave unto the sons of Gershon, according to their service:*

8 *And four wagons and eight oxen he gave unto the sons of Merari, according unto their service, under the hand of Ithamar the son of Aaron the priest.*

9 *But unto the sons of Kohath he gave none: because the service of the sanctuary belonging unto them was that they should bear upon their shoulders.* Num.7:1-9. Some have said that those with whom their load was carried on carts or wagons were ordinary priests, however those who carried the load upon their shoulders were under the anointing, or had a special anointing or prayer called a *gift of the Spirit.* See 1Corinthians 12:8-11 [this becomes a stretch of Scripture]. In other words we are all called to pray but there are those whom are called "prayer warriors", they are the ones carrying the load upon their shoulders.

14 *And this is the confidence that we have in him, that, if we ask any thing according to his will, he heareth us:*

15 *And if we know that he hear us, whatsoever we ask, we know that we have the petitions that we desired of him.* 2Jn.5:14-15.

And when he had taken the book, the four beasts and four and twenty elders fell down before the Lamb, having every one of them harps, and golden vials full of odours, which are the prayers of saints. Rev.5:8. Therefore, as a reminder intercessory prayer is very important and precious to God, as is rises to the very Throne of God and is therefore answered. To fortify this it is important to remember that the Old Testament furnishings were not to be mishandled they were to be carried in a certain manner only by certain persons—the priests and Levites. The New Testament means that only the *born again* are worthy of the priesthood thereby offering intercession for others. The Old Testament Altar of Incense had horns built on the corners meaning that one could hold on to those horns and not let go. The answer was on the way! Likewise today---the answer is on the way! Wait patiently and don't let go!

And Adonijah feared because of Solomon, and arose, and went, and caught hold on the horns of the altar. 1Ki:1:50. When we use the term "hold on to of the horns of the altar" that means we go to God with all of our hearts and cry out for mercy based on the result of what Jesus did when he died on the cross and never let go. It's called persistence!

It is advisable to make a list of those for whom you are praying as it doesn't take many to begin to forget a few. I have a list on my desk at home but sometimes I don't use the list. Many times I pray for someone every time their name crosses my mind. The important thing is that I take everyone seriously and consider it a sacred privilege to pray for them. Therefore I always pray in faith for them believing their answer is on the way. It may not be immediate, but the answer always comes---right on time---God's time. In simple vernacular it means that because I know God hears, I also know He answers.

Sweet smelling savour

15 *For we are unto God a sweet savour of Christ, in them that are saved, and in them that perish:*

> [16] *To the one we are the savour of death unto death; and to the other the savour of life unto life. And who is sufficient for these things?* 2Cor.2:15-16.

Not only are our prayers to be a sweet smelling savor unto God but also our lives as each day we are transformed into the image of Christ. I wonder if I have a body odor to those around me. What is that odor like? Is it pleasing to them or repugnant? What about my prayers to my heavenly Father? Are they filed with repugnant negative complaints and sinful requests or worship and praise?

Comparing the Altar of Incense with Jesus' pattern for prayer

Although Scripture does not indicate the meaning or symbolism for the ingredients used in the incense I can't help but think that somehow Jesus' pattern for prayer in Matthew 6:9-15; Luke 11:1-13 contains the same ingredients as Moses' altar.

i. Adoration for the Father
ii. Forgiveness, Humility
iii. Petition
iv. Deliverance
v. God's will and timing not ours

I notice also that the ingredients aren't measured in equal portions, but crushed, beaten and mixed together indicating the bruising, broken spirit and contriteness of the heart. Psalm 34:18; 51:17; Isaiah 57:15: 66:2. This very same person trembles at God's Word Isaiah 66:2. Is this lacking in our prayers today? Are we not proud and haughty? Do we not need to daily purge and cleanse our dwelling place for the Most High God?

Prayer is not simply a matter of using the correct language rather it is a matter of our heart being right without lust, anger etcetera. It refers not only to the petitioner but also the one interceding. It's good to pray God's word over our situations especially when we don't know how or what to pray, but it's not good to simply recite prayers for the simple reason of availability.

3 *Wherefore have we fasted, say they, and thou seest not? wherefore have we afflicted our soul, and thou takest no knowledge? Behold, in the day of your fast ye find pleasure, and exact all your labours.*

4 *Behold, ye fast for strife and debate, and to smite with the fist of wickedness: ye shall not fast as ye do this day, to make your voice to be heard on high.*

5 *Is it such a fast that I have chosen? a day for a man to afflict his soul? is it to bow down his head as a bulrush, and to spread sackcloth and ashes under him? wilt thou call this a fast, and an acceptable day to the* LORD?

6 *Is not this the fast that I have chosen? to loose the bands of wickedness, to undo the heavy burdens, and to let the oppressed go free, and that ye break every yoke?*

7 *Is it not to deal thy bread to the hungry, and that thou bring the poor that are cast out to thy house? when thou seest the naked, that thou cover him; and that thou hide not thyself*

from thine own flesh? Isa.58:3-7. Even with fasting the addition of pride, strife, debate, wickedness and such like make our prayers unacceptable to God *that He will not and cannot hear Isaiah 59:1-7.*

When properly offered the aroma thereof arose before the Throne of God Revelation 5:8; 8:3, they are the prayers of the saints; our prayers.

Jesus our pattern

With Jesus as our pattern for prayer we must examine His prayers and thus emulate Him.

1. The opening passage was the pattern for the disciples, at their request, and it remains the pattern for the Church of today…it has never changed.
2. All His intercessory prayers were short, many times a word or two rarely more than a short sentence, many times only a word or two! Why? Because He always prayed the Father's will, and in so doing He knew His prayers were always answered.
3. His prayers were packed with power because He always did His Father's will [not His own} John 4:34.
4. The Pharisees said Jesus taught with authority [because when He spoke, things happened].
5. Because His prayers were packed with power they accomplished much and were exact.
6. Likewise the disciples and apostles prayers were brief.
7. Moreover the Creator's word of power is condensed to one word---LET! Genesis 1:3,

6, 9, 11, 14, 15, 20, 24, 26. So Let was the power word followed by a very brief explanation of concise instructions, not a mindless, never ending babble.

Definition of prayer

The abbreviated definition of prayer is summed up as a direct communication with God Almighty Himself. Communication---it takes at least two to have a communication. Communication is a two way street:

1. Dialogue: we pray---God listens. It's not a monolog---it's a dialogue.
2. God answers. It's important to know God's voice---many Christians don't.
3. Prayer is a dialogue not a monologue. It is between two, finite man and his infinite Father.
4. Prayer is HOLY and our Father regards our prayers and petitions of utmost importance.
5. We receive and obey.
6. Prayer is a summons for divine intervention.
7. God speaks, we listen and obey.
8. Prayer, among other things, is the acknowledgement of our personal inadequacy and desperate need for divine intervention. It is humility at its finest.
9. No one wants to listen to an angry, profanity laced tirade, filled with repulsive, vengeful statements. So also our Most High God does not hear us when we "go off on Him". Isaiah58: 1-12 chronicles the difference between hypocritical fasting,

which God will and does not hear and honorable fasting 59:1-8 sates that God will not hear our sinful communications. James 4:1-6 echoes Isaiah's sentiments in that our sinful attitudes block out petitions.

10. Henceforth, when our prayers are consistent in giving respect, honor, adoration, and honor…God hears and answers. That's exactly what Jesus patterned to His disciples when they asked Him to teach them to pray early in His earthly ministry Matthew 6:5-18.

Prayer is a privilege few understand, for it is in prayer we enter into the New Testament priesthood and prophetic ministry. It is prayer that ignites the power of intercession within thus firing up the priesthood. The office of prophet becomes alive when we get an utterance from God to bring to the one for whom we are interceding. When there is a prophetic utterance, also called unction or anointing, in conjunction with prayer, a divine power (anointing) is released that cannot be experienced through the mere flesh of man. This divine power may at times be used in conjunction with one or more of the Spiritual gifts in 1 Corinthians 12:4-11.

- Word of wisdom
- Word of knowledge
- Gifts of healing
- Working of miracles
- Prophecy
- Discerning of spirits
- Diverse kinds of tongues
- Interpretation of tongues

In the New Testament are we become both priest and prophet! But that's no reason to get our dander up, to go stark crazy being overzealous to the point we allow our flesh to overwhelm us and speak or utter nonsense to the party for whom we are interceding. To utter a divine prophecy, or be under the anointing, requires that we listen for the unction or moving of the Spirit within and refuse to utter anything contrary. It is dangerous to utter false statements to anyone saved or unsaved. The utterance from God will, without fail come to pass, but the utterance from the flesh will fail drastically. The Old Testament prophets would rather stand silent than to utter nonsense. They learned to listen for the Spirit. Samuel had a school for the prophets, and although there is little said concerning the school it is evident from Scripture that Samuel focused on discerning God's voice from the voice of the flesh and emotions. It takes the discerning person to be in tune with the anointing. Not everyone has that anointing but everyone should hear His voice John 10:3-8.

We all want people to be healed and their prayers answered but it only comes through the power of the Spirit without which we are just another noise. That's why God's joining His Spirit with ours that we might listen to His voice that power might flow using you and me as vessels of honor.

Some people pray long, lengthy prayers and others seemingly short. It matters not the length only the faith and spirit behind the prayer. Thus true prayer goes beyond mere babblings for it becomes a sweet smelling savor/incense before the Lord on behalf of those for whom we are interceding as well as ourselves Revelation 5:8.

- Remember, we are the New Testament counterparts to the Old Testament priesthood. Therefore we ought the more to be led by the Spirit when interceding for others. Hebrews 9:1-28; 10:1-39 describes the Tabernacle and its furnishings as stand-ins awaiting the reformation of the greater and more perfect tabernacle when Jesus came.
- A part of the priests' duty was to carry the Holy things of the temple either on ox carts provided or upon their own shoulders. They are Holy because they have been consecrated, sanctified and set aside for God's use.
- The Altar of Incense symbolized the New Testament prayer. See Exodus 30:1-10; Numbers 7:1-9. It is this same altar mentioned in Revelation 5:8 called the *prayers of the saints* reminding us that proper prayers become a sweet smelling scent which rise up before the Throne of God thus also implying they are not only heard but also answered.

Knowing your prayers are answered

13 *These things have I written unto you that believe on the name of the Son of God; that ye may know that ye have eternal life, and that ye may believe on the name of the Son of God.*

14 *And this is the confidence that we have in him, that, if we ask any thing according to his will, he heareth us:*

[15] *And if we know that he hear us, whatsoever we ask, we know that we have the petitions that we desired of him.* 1Jn.5:13-15. This is where our faith turns to knowing. Your prayers are answered simply because we believed asking according to His will, not our own. [We just need to "wait for it in patience Romans 8:25.] Simple as that! No more anguishing over and over---you prayed His will---not yours! Therefore you know you have what you prayed for. It's very powerful to know in advance that your prayers are answered even without seeing their manifestation. A synonymous term is---hope. We simply trust His Word on the basis of His character. It is unique only to the Christian faith. No other religion/faith can lay hold of that claim.

- The key is to ask…according to His will…not our own will, but His will, [this means not adding unauthorized or "strange" ingredients to the incense Exodus 30:9].
- A crucial part of His will is that our prayers be consistent with not only Moses' pattern with the Altar of Incense, but also with Jesus' pattern to the disciples Matthew 6:5-18.
- Also God does not respond when we "tell Him what we want Him to do"…we are to "ask Him". So often we're telling Him to do what our flesh wants and not in accordance to His will.
- There becomes a point whereas the knowledge we have goes from mere intellect of the mind to faith or knowing in the heart. That goes for both the intercessor and the seeker. Sometimes the

intercessor has the intellect but lacks the faith or heart to believe.

- So also we can't always agree with someone when their petition is "out of whack"...their heart is also out of alignment with God's will.

How do we know His will from ours? The written Word declares God's will for each of us, therefore when we pray the Word we are praying God's will into our lives. Remember, Jesus said: *For I came down from heaven, not to do mine own will, but the will of him that sent me.* Jn.6:38.

41 *Then they took away the stone from the place where the dead was laid. And Jesus lifted up his eyes, and said, Father, I thank thee that thou hast heard me.*

And I knew that thou hearest me always: but because of the people which stand by, I said it, that they may believe that thou hast sent me. Jn.11:41-42.

- Asking persistently, not letting go of the horns of the altar. [This is not begging it is pleading and making supplication].
- Waiting patiently Romans 8:25.

Persistence in prayer, hold on to the horns of the Altar

The horns on the Altar of Incense represent persistence. Consider every prayer as a weapon whether a knife, arrow, spear, or sword smiting the Goliaths in your life of sickness, disease, financial, moral, mental, relational, financial, physical, emotional.

- As long as you're still praying…you haven't given up!
- As long as someone is praying for you…don't give up!
- If you are interceding for another…don't give up!
- If you're fighting many giants simultaneously…don't give up!
- As long as your prayers are consistent with God's pattern, mentioned above…don't give up!
- Call on those warriors who will champion your cause…don't give up!
- Make sure those who intercede for you truly believe.

Our Lord gives us so many diverse ways to get answers to prayer. When your request does not come, either try another manner, below, or examine your prayer ingredients. If you find "strange ingredients" humbly confess and repent of them and proceed with the proper ingredients.

- One on one all by ourselves. Abraham prayed persistently for his nephew Lot and his family in Sodom Genesis 18:16-33.
- Two or three agreeing together. The power of agreement. Aaron and Hur held up Moses' hands when he grew weary and prevailed in war over Amalek, Exodus 17:8-13.

- Corporate prayer: the church prayed for Peter's release from jail Acts 12:1-18.
- Praying in the Spirit Romans 8:25-26; calms the flesh, and summons divine power. Prayer and fasting, Isaiah 58:1-12. Patience; often missed because we are used to getting our miracles, healing and answers to prayer NOW! Romans 8:25b.
- Child like prayer: *But Jesus said, Suffer little children, and forbid them not, to come unto me: for of such is the kingdom of heaven.* Matt.19:14.

Jesus said: [19]*Again I say unto you, That if two of you shall agree on earth as touching any thing that they shall ask, it shall be done for them of my Father which is in heaven.*

[20] *For where two or three are gathered together in my name, I am there in the midst of them.* Matt.18:19-20. Unity in prayer is like an army against the enemy. I count it a blessing when someone tells me they are praying for me.

Belief and faith

[20] *And in the morning, as they passed by, they saw the fig tree dried up from the roots.*

21 *And Peter calling to remembrance saith unto him, Master, behold, the fig tree which thou cursedst is withered away.*

[22] *And Jesus answering saith unto them, Have faith in God.* Our faith is to be in God, not ourselves.

23 *For verily I say unto you, That whosoever shall say unto this mountain, Be thou removed, and be thou cast into the sea; and shall not doubt in his heart, but shall believe that those things which he saith shall come to pass; he shall have whatsoever he saith.* How can a man declare a mountain be removed without first having made the decision that it can be? Doubt is indecisiveness the decision simply has not been made--- it's still in the mulling over stage.

24 *Therefore I say unto you, What things soever ye desire, when ye pray, believe that ye receive them, and ye shall have them.* When, not after, you pray.

25 *And when ye stand praying, forgive, if ye have ought against any: that your Father also which is in heaven may forgive you your trespasses.*

26 *But if ye do not forgive, neither will your Father which is in heaven forgive your trespasses.* Mk.11:20-26.

Belief and faith are required before any petition is uttered. Both are the result of a decision made based on rock solid evidence.

- A person is absolutely convinced beyond a shadow of doubt before the prayer is uttered. Time and again Jesus presented rock solid evidence of His deity, His love, His compassion and both His ability, desire and willingness to heal answer prayers and slay all our *Goliath* giants. When He walked this earth He presented tangible undisputed evidence…but now He gives us His Word as rock solid evidence Matthew 14:31; 21:21; John 3:16-18; Romans 10:8-12; Jas.1:8; 4:8.

John 20:19-31 chronicles the story of "doubting Thomas" who when in the upper room with the disciples, after Jesus' death, refused to believe until he had seen the nail prints in Jesus' hands. Jesus reprimanded him saying "*Thomas, because thou hast seen me, thou hast believed: blessed are they that have not seen me, and yet have believed*". This speaks of the contemporary church. We are to make decisions based on the Word we see and hear without physical evidence not only of salvation but also healing and deliverance as well as any request we have. This goes, I believe, double for the intercessor.

Unanswered prayer

Could it be?

Could it be that our prayers go unanswered because we have somehow been guilty of any of the following?
Each element for the aroma has been carefully selected by God to produce the proper sweet smelling aroma thus assurance of answered prayers, therefore have we begun to:

- Take prayer for granted?
- Have we substituted or added to the various elements necessary to produce the required aroma with a pungent producing element such as sin, jealousy, anger or such like?
  [9]*Ye shall offer no strange incense thereon, nor burnt sacrifice, nor meat offering; neither shall ye pour drink offering thereon.* Ex.30:9.

- I've often heard it said that God arbitrarily chose not to answer this or that prayer for no apparent reason. That stands in stark contrast to His promises to answer the desires of our hearts and watch over His Word to perform it.
- It has also been stated that God answers all prayers regardless. That's untrue for Isaiah 59:1-8 that God cannot hear requests because of iniquity coming between them/us and God and James 4:1-7 that God resists the proud and gives grace to the humble and answers not the prayers of the lustful and greedy

- Pay close attention to Jesus pattern for prayer in Matthew 6:5-15; Luke 11:1-13.
- Or perhaps we've let go of the horns of the Altar too soon, persistence…or maybe never took hold of the horns.
    - How long do I pray for something/hold on to the horns of the altar? Answer: until your answer comes! Until then HANG ON don't let go, don't give up![It may come in a manner we're not expecting.]
- Maybe, just maybe, we can't decide what we want and vacillate between.
    - Do I want to be healed?
    - Or do I want to just get along the best I can…we muse?
    - Or…do I just want to die now and get it over…I'm sick and tired.

As we muse these and more we must ask ourselves…Is God really that fickle? We surely must

know we can't have everything and He simply isn't that gullible as to give us, as a child's Christmas wish list to Santa…it contradicts the WORD.
I think perhaps the answer might be…Let thy will, not mine be done Lord.

All the furnishings had golden rings in the sides for the staves to be inserted that the priests might move them whenever the Tabernacle was to be moved. As New Testament believers, we are to take the gospel message [furnishings], God's Word, wherever we go…into all the world Acts 1:8 which speaks of divine empowerment once the Holy Ghost has come upon us thus uniting with our spirit 1Corinthians 6:17 making us one.

Jesus taught the disciples how to pray in Matthew 6:5-15, Luke 11:1-13 which ought to give it great significance. Upon closer examination Jesus' pattern for prayer is not unlike Moses' Altar of Incense including the ingredients for incense.

- Adoration and glory to the Father
- Praise and worship
- Petition for needs
- Humility---forgiveness
- All these like the Old Testament were to be crushed and mixed together as a sweet smelling fragrance.

  - Notice the absence of malice, sin, vengeance, wrath, un-forgiveness, lust, etcetera which would make the prayers a repugnant odor thus unacceptable. See Isaiah 58:1-14; Colossians 3:5-16; James 4:1-3

The New Testament saints put a lot of emphasis in prayer for they knew it was the summoning of divine power and intervention into their lives as well as those for whom they interceded. If the disciples had known how to pray then they had no need to ask Jesus for instructions.

It could be said that New Testament prayer is interceding for another like the Old Testament priest offering sacrifices for the one who could not on his/her own.

Sin

Scripture gives three (3) reasons for unanswered prayers which also constitute wrongful ingredients added to the incense.

1. Iniquity/lawlessness: [1]*Behold, the LORD's hand is not shortened, that it cannot save; neither his ear heavy, that it cannot hear:*

   [2]*But your iniquities have separated between you and your God, and your sins have hid his face from you, that he will not hear.*

   [3]*For your hands are defiled with blood, and your fingers with iniquity; your lips have spoken lies, your tongue hath muttered perverseness.*

   [4]*None calleth for justice, nor any pleadeth for truth: they trust in vanity, and speak lies; they conceive mischief, and bring forth iniquity.* Isa.59:1-4.

2. Lust/sin: [1]*From whence come wars and fightings among you? come they not hence, even of your lusts that war in your members?*

[2]*Ye lust, and have not: ye kill, and desire to have, and cannot obtain: ye fight and war, yet ye have not, because ye ask not.*

[3]*Ye ask, and receive not, because ye ask amiss, that ye may consume it upon your lusts.*

[4]*Ye adulterers and adulteresses, know ye not that the friendship of the world is enmity with God? whosoever therefore will be a friend of the world is the enemy of God.* Jas.3:1-4. David's son died because he lusted after Bathsheba sent her husband to the front lines to be killed and attempted to cover it up. 2Samuel 11:2-27; 12:12-25. David knew better.
   - In other words unanswered prayers are caused by our own sinful attitudes and sin itself thus adding a strange ingredient to our prayers, thus making them unanswerable and unacceptable to God according to His standards. Even when we fast and pray not just any fast is acceptable to God see Isaiah 58:1-14.

3. Not persevering: *Pray without ceasing.* 1Thess.5:17. [As represented by the horns on the altar]. Sometimes I think I get complacent in prayer and let go of the horns of the altar.

[7] *Ask, and it shall be given you; seek, and ye shall find; knock, and it shall be opened unto you:*

[8] For every one that asketh receiveth; and he that seeketh findeth; and to him that knocketh it shall be opened

[9] Or what man is there of you, whom if his son ask bread, will he give him a stone?

[10] Or if he ask a fish, will he give him a serpent?

[11] If ye then, being evil, know how to give good gifts unto your children, how much more shall your Father which is in heaven give good things to them that ask him?

[12] Therefore all things whatsoever ye would that men should do to you, do ye even so to them: for this is the law and the prophets Matt.7:7-12.

And Adonijah feared because of Solomon, and arose, and went, and caught hold on the horns of the altar. 1KI.1:50. The brazen altar is where the sacrifices were slain 1 Kings 1:50-51. A fugitive taking hold of the horns in effect was pleading for asylum and mercy. The Altar of Incense, Exodus 37:25; Leviticus 4:7, 18, is where the prayers of the saints were offered. Although it's considered inconclusive by many scholars, taking hold of these horns represented persistence until the prayer was answered.

Today, we are to be persistent in our petitions, 2 Thessalonians 5:17; Matthew 7:7-11; Mark 11:22-26; Luke 11:8-13. A lack or persistence is tantamount to unbelief or doubting.

Divine delays; How long O Lord

Quite often we're faced with the question; "How long O Lord until you answer my prayer?" Psalm 13:1-2 records David pleaded four times "How Long, Lord". Divine delays are confused with unanswered prayer, when in fact they are two different things. The question of God's prolonged response is well documented in Scripture. God waited 430 years before sending Moses to deliver Israel from bondage.

Scripture records numerous divine delays: 1 Samuel I 1-28 Hannah's prayer; Psalm 6:3; 13: 1; 69:3; 130:5-6, five times;119:82; John 11:-17 when Jesus was derided for delaying His plea to come pray for Lazarus. Patience is admonished in James 5:7; 2Peter 2:9 exhorts us that *The Lord is not slack concerning His promise…but is longsuffering to us-ward.* It's a matter of patience.

Psalm 37:7 *Rest in the Lord, and wait patiently for Him: fret not thyself because oh him who prospereth in his way, because of the man who bringeth wicked devices to pass.*

Psalm 40:1 *I waited patiently for the Lord: and He inclined unto me, and heard my cry.* Resting and waiting seems to me an international malady. We wait "patiently" for the waiter, for the bus or train, for the cashier. But are we truly patient as we glibly remind ourselves how busy other people are. And yet waiting patiently for the Lord appears to be a prerequisite.

Waiting on the Lord is but a part of His development and maturing of our personal faith. When He delays, and He often does, it serves to deepen our trust in Him. 1Peter 1:3-9 speaks of our faith being tried as gold through much temptation, *receiving the end of our faith, the salvation of our souls.*

Although we may not like it the end result is worth far more than our *light affliction.*

Dying in faith without receiving the promise

Hebrews 11 is often called the "Faith Hall of Fame" known for its accounts of faithful saints of old and their walks of faith. Verses 33-37 describe many who endured many things including beatings, lions dens, fiery furnaces, cruel mocking, scourged, stoning, being sawn into pieces such like. However verses 38-40 tell a different story, of those being tormented, homeless, wandering in a wilderness and dying in faith without obtaining their promise. God still accounted their living as faith. So also there are those who pray earnestly in faith whom God counts as faithful. I think perhaps we ought to be more cautious whom we label as "faithless" when God counts them as faithful. God's accounting of faithfulness far outweighs man's feeble accounting.

Even if---God is able

Daniel 3:17-18 *If it be so, our God whom we serve is able to deliver us from the burning fiery furnace, and He will deliver us out of thine hand, O King.*

18*But if not,* [if God chooses not to heal or deliver me] *be it known unto thee O king, that we* [I]*will not serve thy gods, not worship the golden image* [nor refuse to believe and serve the living God] *that thou hast set up.* Although we're not healed or delivered the Lord our God still wants us to hold on to the horns of the altar in firm belief in His ability to heal or deliver.

God is in control, His timing

Hebrews 4:15-16 *For we have not an high priest which cannot be touched with the feeling of our infirmities; but was in all points tempted like as we are. Yet without sin.*

16 *Let us therefore come boldly unto the throne of grace, that we might obtain mercy, and find grace to help in time of need.* See also, 2Thessalonians 3:16-18. When we feel like we can't go any father, we've done all we can, and we feel like giving up…His grace is enough to sustain us. His grace brings about a peace to our soul that's impossible to comprehend. We haven't given up we've simply gone to a higher level in faith. Romans 1:17a tells us, *For therein is the righteousness of God revealed from faith to faith.* As we travail in this broken world, though we see not our petitions answered in our expectations of time, yet we are still growing *from faith to faith.* God Himself is still in control and we must embrace it. We simply cannot manipulate Him.

Bottom line

The bottom line is that God never ever violates His own written or spoken Word. From time to time someone will say. "God said no to my prayer." The truth is that God will never say no to a request if it hasn't violated at least one of the above mentioned reasons. He is in the business of answering prayer not denying them. Fact is, some prayers will take longer due to the nature of the request, or perhaps our Heavenly Father is teaching us patience, understanding, love or any number of things critical to our spiritual health and well being. For example: relationship requests often take longer because now He has to touch more than one heart, others He takes longer because a "heart condition" needs changing. Not to mention our own heart may be hardened and in need of extensive "work in progress".

So what is His will? Don't add unauthorized ingredients to the incense.

God's will for prayer is outlined in James 4:2-5:

[1] *From whence come wars and fightings among you? come they not hence, even of your lusts that war in your members?*

[2] *Ye lust, and have not: ye kill, and desire to have, and cannot obtain: ye fight and war, yet ye have not, because ye ask not.*

[3] *Ye ask, and receive not, because ye ask amiss, that ye may consume it upon your lusts.*

[4] *Ye adulterers and adulteresses, know ye not that the friendship of the world is enmity with God? whosoever therefore will be a friend of the world is the enemy of God.*

[5] *Do ye think that the scripture saith in vain, The spirit that dwelleth in us lusteth to envy?*

- There is a battle waging within one's own heart.
- Attempting to have one's own way without seeking divine guidance.
- Asking to fulfill an evil lust within one's heart.
- A lustful spirit within.

[2]*But your iniquities have separated between you and your God, and your sins have hid* **his** *face from you, that he will not hear.* Isa.59:2.

- Isaiah states that iniquity [lawlessness] not merely an act of sin but the attitude of one's heart toward God's law and man's.

Anything outside of a good conscience toward God is not His will and therefore we are assured He will not hear our prayers.

A word to the wise

Not everyone operates under the same anointing just as not everyone has all the gifts of the Spirit. However, it is vital for the entire body of Christ be trained to operate in the gift they are given. Again it is for the benefit if the entire body and not simply that individual. An excellent resource is *Strongman's His Name…What's His Game* by Carol & Jerry Robeson.

Praying in the Spirit

Surely after studying the Altar of Incense we can readily understand that it is the Spirit creating that sweet smelling aroma before the Throne, Revelation 8:5.

22 *For we know that the whole creation groaneth and travaileth in pain together until now.*

23 *And not only they, but ourselves also, which have the firstfruits of the Spirit, even we ourselves groan within ourselves, waiting for the adoption, to wit, the redemption of our body.* Rom.8:22-23. The passage takes us back to the Old Testament whereas creation became infected with the same ill effects of the fall *groaning and traviling in pain.*

Thus verse 23 demonstrates that our spirits are likewise groaning though we have the *Firstfruits of the Spirit* we also anxiously await the redemption not only of our bodies but also of the whole creation. For the most part it is understood that praying in the Spirit is in fact praying in an unknown tongue. We have no understanding of what we are praying but the Spirit does and intercedes on our behalf. However, it may also be praying in your common language under the anointing or moving of the Spirit.

[26] *Likewise the Spirit also helpeth our infirmities: for we know not what we should pray for as we ought: but the Spirit itself maketh intercession for us with groanings which cannot be uttered* .

> [27] *And he that searcheth the hearts knoweth what is the mind of the Spirit, because he maketh intercession for the saints according to the will of God.* Rom.8:26-27. Many times we find it difficult to pray God's will in our lives. It ought to be a great consolation to us that The Spirit has an edge on us knowing God's will. Therefore we ought the more be ready to pray in the Spirit. The Spirit Himself is interceding for you and I when we pray in the Spirit. God's got it all covered! Praying in the Spirit calms the flesh, and emotions, stabilizes the mind and soul clears the way for summoning divine intervention. It's a vital weapon in spiritual warfare.

What if I can't pray?

Finding oneself with the inability to pray could signal any one of several things.

- You are steeped deep in iniquity so that God cannot and will not hear you.
- You are not a child of God aka *born again.*
- Unbelief.
- Deeply focused on issues rather than on Him.
- The remedy is to ask God to help you pray, even though it be praying in the Spirit.

Why is prayer so important?

The importance of prayer cannot be overstated for it is the summoning of divine assistance in, quite literally, every issue of life.

- Without the privilege of prayer we are doomed to a life of failure bouncing from one bad decision to another without learning and benefiting from one's mistakes.
- Without the benefits of prayer we are just like every other "faith" seesawing back and forth without solid answers upon which to rely.
- We all desperately need divine guidance for the issues of life whether great or small.
- Prayer is in fact spiritual warfare! Perhaps this is why prayer can be so tedious, boring, and wearisome at times.

Can we not see from the dialogue between God and Cain that God is attempting to reach Cain with love not condemnation?

[4]*And Abel, he also brought of the firstlings of his flock and of the fat thereof. And the Lord had respect unto Abel and to his offering:*

[5]*But unto Cain and to his offering he had not respect. And Cain was very wroth, and his countenance fell.*

[6]*And the Lord said unto Cain, Why art thou wroth? and why is thy countenance fallen?*

[7]*If thou doest well, shalt thou not be accepted? And if thou doest not well, sin lieth at the door. And unto thee shall be his desire, and thou shalt rule over him.*

[8]*And Cain talked with Abel his brother: and it came to pass, when they were in the field, that Cain rose up against Abel his brother, and slew him.*

[9]*And the Lord said unto Cain, Where is Abel thy brother? And he said, I know not: Am I my brother's keeper?*
[10]*And he said, What hast thou done? the voice of thy brother's blood crieth unto me from the ground.*

[11]*And now art thou cursed from the earth, which hath opened her mouth to receive thy brother's blood from thy hand;*

[12]*When thou tillest the ground, it shall not henceforth yield unto thee her strength; a fugitive and a vagabond shalt thou be in the earth.*

[13]*And Cain said unto the Lord, My punishment is greater than I can bear.*

[14]*Behold, thou hast driven me out this day from the face of the earth; and from thy face shall I be hid; and I shall be a fugitive and a vagabond in the earth; and it shall come to pass, that every one that findeth me shall slay me.*

[15]*And the Lord said unto him, Therefore whosoever slayeth Cain, vengeance shall be taken on him sevenfold. And the Lord set a mark upon Cain, lest any finding him should kill him.*

[16]*And Cain went out from the presence of the Lord, and dwelt in the land of Nod, on the east of Eden.* Gen.4:4-16. Abel's offering had the Lord's respect as opposed to his brother Cain, who's offering had not the Lord's respect. The difference…the heart, one was evil, Cain, while the other, Abel, had thoughts of life and spiritual matters.

Then Jacob gave Esau bread and pottage of lentils; and he did eat and drink, and rose up, and went his way: thus Esau despised his birthright. Gen.25:3. Self explanatory…Esau despised or hated the *birthright* which is but another term for iniquity or lawlessness.

Benefits of the giants in our lives

Yes, although it's difficult to comprehend, sometimes the giants in our lives can benefit us; we can learn much from our giants.

- Comforts
- Strengthens
- Encourages
- Heals
- Builds confidence, faith, hope and patience (Romans 5:4; James 1:2-4)
- [10] *The name of the LORD is a strong tower: the righteous runneth into it, and is safe.* Pro.18:10.

Humble yourself

This means asking according to God's pattern both with Moses and Jesus. That's humbling because we have to get our flesh out of the way by using

God's pattern. Note: both Moses' and Jesus' patterns are the exact same.

12*And the LORD appeared to Solomon by night, and said unto him, I have heard thy prayer, and have chosen this place to myself for an house of sacrifice.*

13 *If I shut up heaven that there be no rain, or if I command the locusts to devour the land, or if I send pestilence among my people;*

14 *If my people, which are called by my name, shall humble themselves, and pray, and seek my face, and turn from their wicked ways; then will I hear from heaven, and will forgive their sin, and will heal their land.*

15*Now mine eyes shall be open, and mine ears attend unto the prayer that is made in this place.*

16*For now have I chosen and sanctified this house, that my name may be there forever: and mine eyes and mine heart shall be there perpetually.* 2Chron.7:12-16. After Solomon's prayer, the glory of God filling the Temple, that the priests could not enter; God spoke to Solomon declaring:

- The Temple was chosen to be a house of prayer and sacrifice. Today we are God's Temple and we are to pray and offer the sacrifices of praise and thanksgiving. Each believer is a house of prayer! The church collectively is also a house of prayer.

Four requirements a believer must do for God to answer

1. Each believer is to humble themselves. For some it may seem difficult.
2. Pray…it is a humbling task to pray as it takes humility to pray and leave results to another.
3. Seek God's face…speaks of intimacy, trust, respect, dependence.
4. Turn from wicked ways…repent. Sometimes this is the hardest to do as we are so caught up in out sin. It's not because God has decided ambiguously to not answer your prayer/s. Isaiah 59:2 *But your iniquities have separated between you and your God, and your sins have hid his face from you, that he will not hear.* God has specifics we must follow to receive answers…perhaps the most neglected is that of our wickedness.

- Sinful habits become strongholds which often require outside help from another believer.
- We may also ask God to deliver us from sinful habits or addictions.
- He does not arbitrarily chose not to answer…there is always a solid reason…sin.

Intercessory Prayer

It's called intercessory prayer because others join you in your personal battles and struggles of life to encourage, strengthen, uplift, pray, admonish and hold up your weary hands toward heaven to secure your victory. Or vice-versa you may be called upon to intercede for another. Many times it will be an extended, prolonged battle, enough to weaken you, if possible, but it will be worth it in the sometimes verrry loooong run! Either way the victory will be well worth the battle

Suggestions for prayer

- 1 minute prayer: a designated person relays prayer requests to others who pray for one minute. Works great as many cannot commit to longer times.
- 24 hour prayer: for those who can commit to longer prayers. Many times shifts are designated.
- Proxy: it's not always necessary or feasible for the person to be present, so having a stand in is appropriate.
- Two or three gathered together. [20] *For where two or three are gathered together in my name, there am I in the midst of them.* Matt.18:20.
- Spontaneous, many times in the Spirit. [26] *Likewise the Spirit also helpeth our infirmities: for we know not what we should pray for as we ought: but the Spirit itself maketh intercession for us with groanings which cannot be uttered.*
- Invite many to pray for you until the answer comes…bombard the Throne of God.

[27] *And he that searcheth the hearts knoweth what is the mind of the Spirit, because he maketh intercession for the saints according to the will of God.* Rom.8:26-27. Very powerful for the flesh is stilled and quieted allowing and summoning the Spirit's power to work.

Conclusion

In conclusion, if a man's heart is set on evil, iniquity and lawlessness it is no wonder he is not able to pray or receive answers. If a man has a heart for God his prayer will be answered… eventually, in His timing…not ours. The tenant that God answers prayers immediately runs counter to Scripture. Prayer is not a drive up window where one can acquire their "quick fix" in thirty seconds. And it's not a lack of faith…most likely it's a Divine Delay.

When God's warriors go down on their knees, the battle is not over, it has just begun". Michael Orona

Chapter 2

Anointing Oil

As with examining the Old Testament one must take caution not to put too much emphasis on keeping the Law as it will surely lead to legalism and departure from the spirit of the Law. Our Lord is far more interested in the heart condition than which physical ingredients are the composition of the Anointing Oil. We have studied the Altar of Incense, its structure and elements of the incense and their meaning without, hopefully implying that one must need to construct a physical altar like unto Moses. Clearly it appears that our Lord is far more interested in our heart than whether we use olive oil or the exact ingredients as opposed to WD40, 10w30 or another composition for the purpose of anointing simply because the New Testament does not clearly specify the composition for such oil; one must assume that the New Testament saints knew and clearly followed its concise specification.

Anointing oil used for the anointing of the Tabernacle, and Temple furniture had a composition separate from the New Testament, which appears to be pure olive oil. The oil from the olive is more than 50% of the ripe olive. It was crushed either in a stone press or bare feet. The olive oil had various uses such as cooking oil, dietary supplement, a medicinal balm, or for use as a fuel for a lamp. The Ten Virgins Matthew 25:1-13 used oil in their lamps. It is often referred to as a 'type of the Holy Spirit'.

Anointing Oil usage

Originally the anointing oil was to be used for the ordination of the priests and the High Priest, the Tabernacle and its furnishings but later for the prophets and kings 1Samuel 10:1. It was forbidden for use on strangers or a person's body [this ointment is sacred, holy and not to be used for personal use as a perfume or deodorant nor for any stranger or unbeliever…it is holy]. It was also used for hospitality and courtesy toward a guest Psalm.92:10; Ecclesiates.9:8.

- The woman who washed Jesus' feet using ointment and wiped His feet with her hair in Luke 7:36-38. It was an ancient custom of hospitality. It was very expensive.
- Jesus washed the disciples' feet before His arrest. John 13:1-12.

22 *Moreover the LORD spake unto Moses, saying,*

23 *Take thou also unto thee principal spices, of pure myrrh five hundred shekels, and of sweet cinnamon half so much, even two hundred and fifty shekels, and of sweet calamus two hundred and fifty shekels,*

24 *And of cassia five hundred shekels, after the shekel of the sanctuary, and of oil olive an hin:*

[25] *And thou shalt make it an oil of holy ointment, an ointment compound after the art of the apothecary: it shall be an holy anointing oil.*

[26] *And thou shalt anoint the tabernacle of the congregation therewith, and the ark of the testimony,*

[27] *And the table and all his vessels, and the candlestick and his vessels, and the altar of incense,*

[28] *And the altar of burnt offering with all his vessels, and the laver and his foot.*

[29] *And thou shalt sanctify them, that they may be most holy: whatsoever toucheth them shall be holy.*

[30] *And thou shalt anoint Aaron and his sons, and consecrate them, that they may minister unto me in the priest's office.*

[31] *And thou shalt speak unto the children of Israel, saying, This shall be an holy anointing oil unto me throughout your generations.*

[32] *Upon man's flesh shall it not be poured, neither shall ye make any other like it, after the composition of it: it is holy, and it shall be holy unto you.*

[33] *Whosoever compoundeth any like it, or whosoever putteth any of it upon a stranger, shall even be cut off from his people.* Ex.30:22-33.

Anointing oil ingredients

Pure Myrrh, sweet cinnamon, cassia, olive oil, and kaneh bosem (Ex.30:23). To be mixed together into an apothecary. In contrast to the incense for the Altar of Incense each ingredient was to be a certain measure thus enhancing the ointment. The significance of the ingredients is unknown, however, when mixed together it was a sweet smelling savour.

The Christian church has continued using oil for anointing, however, its compound varies differently from Moses' day. Unfortunately it is produced commercially for profit ignoring its intrinsic values. Mostly, I presume, it consists of olive oil but certainly not the original compound.

Today it is used in conjunction with the laying on of hands James 5:14-16 whereas the sick may call on the elders of the church to anoint them that they might be healed. Sins are also forgiven in such cases. Confession of sins is also admonished. In many churches a person is designated to operate on a prayer team usually after services.

Type of the Holy Spirit's presence

Numerous passages come to mind, Matthew 25 1-10 the 10 virgins with lamps trimmed with and without oil typifies the Holy Spirit's presence. Likewise it ought to be used in a holy manner. There is nothing magical about the oil, only in its significance to the presence of God.

- Psalm 133:2 equates the unity of the brethren with the oil/ointment poured on Aaron, the High Priest's head running down his beard and his garments…a type of the Spirit's presence.

The reality is that you will grieve forever. You will not get over the loss of a loved one; you will learn to live with it. You will heal and you will rebuild yourself around the loss you have suffered. You will be whole again but you will never be the same, nor should you want to.

Chapter 3

Armor, Protection, Weapons of War [the Christian's Armory]

Far too often Christians attempt spiritual warfare in the flesh without being properly trained in spiritual warfare. Every day we need to stop at the armory and ready ourselves for the day at hand.

[10] *Finally, my brethren, be strong in the Lord, and in the power of his might.*

[11] *Put on the whole armour of God, that ye may be able to stand against the wiles of the devil.*

[12] *For we wrestle not against flesh and blood, but against principalities, against powers, against the rulers of the darkness of this world, against spiritual wickedness in high places.* This is spiritual warfare too often disguising itself as natural.

[13] *Wherefore take unto you the whole armour of God, that ye may be able to withstand in the evil day, and having done all, to stand.* God provides for us to stand and prevail…are we taking advantage of that or did we go off to war without putting on our full armor?

[14] *Stand therefore, having your loins girt about with truth, and having on the breastplate of righteousness;* TRUTH.

[15] *And your feet shod with the preparation of the gospel of peace;* PEACE. Peace with God; not anger or vengeance.

[16] *Above all, taking the shield of faith, wherewith ye shall be able to quench all the fiery darts of the wicked.* FAITH.

[17] *And take the helmet of salvation, and the sword of the Spirit, which is the word of God:* GOD'S WORD, SALVATION. One simply cannot be victorious in spiritual warfare without having first been saved.

[18] *Praying always with all prayer and supplication in the Spirit, and watching thereunto with all perseverance and supplication for all saints;* Eph.6:10-18. PRAYER.

Have you ever heard of an army without weapons or armor? Every army trains for combat in the use of armor, for defense, and weapons for offensive fighting. As Christians we are enlisted in the Lord's army and need to be aware of our weapons and armor and trained in their usage. This is a critical chapter to absorb for it not only familiarizes one with their weapons but is set to train you in their usage to your advantage. Another critical topic is Hearing God's Voice for Christians must learn their Father's voice just as a child yearns to hear the voice of their parents.

Definition revisited. The *birthright* is the right which naturally belonged to the *firstborn* son; very plain and simple but not without its peculiar complications. As God's children it is imperative that we clearly understand our *birthrights,* for this section tackles but a few of those *birthrights* that have eluded the church for so long. Remember, Jesus has preeminence in the *birthright* and shares His inheritance with us. For no other reason than simplicity I have chosen to pen them alphabetically.

Just as Israel had weapons of bows and arrows, spears, and swords so also does the church of today; the difference is that ours are spiritual, more powerful than their physical weapons. The Lord has given us so many weapons for warfare it's almost unfathomable.

Whole Armour of God [not just part of it]

[13]*Wherefore take unto you the whole armour of God that ye may be able to withstand in the evil day, and having done all, to stand.* Evil days come upon us all. Our Great God has provided all we need to stand no matter what.

[14]*Stand therefore, having your loins girt about with truth, and having on the breastplate of righteousness;* Truthfulness stands apart from untruth and will reveal our every weakness. The Breastplate of righteousness is given when our Heavenly Father declares us righteous for our new found faith in Christ.

[15]*And your feet shod with the preparation of the gospel of peace;* Peace gives us our marching orders, not violence. Peace also means that we are no longer enemies of God, for peace is established by the blood of Jesus Christ. There is a peace in the midst of turmoil given by God to withstand even the most hideous of circumstances.

[16]*Above all, taking the shield of faith wherewith ye shall be able to quench all the fiery darts of the wicked. Faith,* our trust in Him and all His promises will stop all evil

from harming us. Though sickness, disease and adversity and evil of all sorts assail us yet our souls remain steadfast.

[17]*And take the helmet of salvation, and the sword of the Spirit, which is the word of God.* The helmet reminds all or our great salvation, protecting our minds, and hearts and the sword is used as an offensive weapon and defensive armor to be used discreetly being well trained in its usage.

[18]*Praying always with all prayer and supplication in the Spirit, and watching thereunto with all perseverance and supplication for all saints;* Eph.6:13-18. Yes, prayer is a vital part of our armor as it beckons the armies of the Heavenly Host to war against our enemies thus securing out victories.

1. Weapons are spiritual not carnal 2Corinthians 10:3-6 they are mighty, pull down strongholds, dispel vain ideas and thoughts, captivate our evil thoughts causing us to obey Him, and bring revenge on the disobedient.
2. Refuge, cities of: Numbers 35:6; Psalms 59:10-17 the name of the Lord is a strong tower [we can run to our refuge in Him whenever the need].
3. Prayer: Luke 11:1-13 [Jesus knew <u>without a doubt</u> His prayers were answered, so do we!] [If you don't <u>know</u> then what's the sense of praying?] 1John 5:14-15 …*if we*

ask…according to His will…He heareth us…[15] *…and if we know He hears us…we know we have the petitions we desired.* Even praying in the Spirit/tongues as it calms our fleshly emotions, soul, mind, and spirit and garrisons the angelic host to secure our victory.

4. Fasting and prayer: Isaiah 58:1-14; 61:3. To lose the bands/chains of wickedness and set us free!
5. Confession: 1Jn. 1:9-10. Acknowledging sin for what it is…calling it for what it is…taking responsibility and ownership for our sin.
6. Repentance: turning away; [a 180 turn in the opposite direction; many of us have not turned away from sin, thereby increasing our struggles with sin]. It is the Siamese twin of confession.
7. Casting down of imaginations: 2Corinthians 10:3-3. Many times our imaginations can run wild.
8. Renewed thinking: Philippians 4:4-9
9. Resistance: resist the devil and he will flee James.4:7. Our tendency is to charge headlong into spiritual battles with our feeble flesh.
10. As in the Old Testament God often fought battles with both a

heavenly host as well as human soldiers. Likewise He uses still His heavenly, unseen, armies, but also has ordained human authority in the form of political leaders, federal, state, and local in the executive, legislative and judicial branches, military, and civilian law enforcement see Romans 13:1-6.

11. Praying in tongues aka praying in the Spirit Romans 8: 26-27. It calms and soothes the flesh and emotions, encourages, fortifies, and strengthens the spirit, soul, and mind while summoning divine power to bring forth victory.
12. To awake from our slumber. Enter the world without our armor is akin to leaving the house buck naked without our clothes exposing our nether parts to the evil elements, risking arrest and even more drastic and dramatic wounds. It's like playing football without the proper padding, training, practice and coaching.

Note: When we are trying to resist something, and we all do at some point in our lives, many of us have the propensity to dabble, entertain, or toy with the evilness; that's why the devil won't flee from us. Instead he has taken us captive or captivated us in whatever evil it happens to be. As a result those very thoughts, desires, and inclinations ultimately taking us captive like dumb sheep to the slaughter.

a) The following passages will help us to resist:

I. *No condemnation.* Rom.8:1.

II. *No temptation taken you.* 1Cor.10:13.

III. *I die daily.* 1Cor.15:31

IV. *casting down imaginations*…2Cor.10:2-6

V. Philippians 4:6-9 change your thinking

VI. Colossians 3:5-15 the great put off and put on…mortify, crucify the deeds of the flesh

VII. *every man is tempted.* Jas.1:12-15.

VIII. *resist the devil and he will flee from you*…Jas.4:7.

IX. Sin, when given opportunity, grows, to incapacitate the Christian causing fear, self dis-fellowshipping with God and fellow believers, and study of His Word. One simply cannot be obedient to His Word if he or she does not know the Word or consistently immerse themselves it the Word. Note: this does not mean one has lost their salvation only that their walk with God is impaired thus stunting their growth and delaying certain blessings because of sin's work within.

[9] *Wherewithal shall a young man cleanse his way? By taking heed thereto according to thy word.*

[10] *With my whole heart have I sought thee: O let me not wander from thy commandments.*

[11] *Thy word have I hid in mine heart, that I might not sin against thee.* Ps.119:9-11.

Note: The only reason the devil doesn't flee is that we really <u>aren't trying</u> to resist…we are entertaining and toying the evil thoughts and inclinations. As a result those very thoughts, desires, and inclinations ultimately <u>take us captive</u> like dumb sheep to the slaughter. As James 1:14-15 states the evil thoughts eventually become reality when rehearsed for extended periods of time which eventually lead to physically carrying out those evil imaginations. The end result is death. We simply cannot fight these battles on our own. The Spirit freely provides all the help we need to not only win the battles of life but also the war!

Do this and you will keep the Lord's temple pure, cleansed, and holy. Remember and review the life of Joseph. It is our Heavenly Father's desire not only to save us but also to cleanse us daily; it is but a part of our transformation.

Spiritual warfare

2 *But I beseech* **you**, *that I may not be bold when I am present with that confidence, wherewith I think to be bold against some, which think of us as if we walked according to the flesh.* The Word will give us boldness and confidence.

3 *For though we walk in the flesh, we do not war after the flesh:*

4 *(For the weapons of our warfare* **are** *not carnal, but mighty through God to the pulling down of strong holds;)*

5 *Casting down imaginations, and every high thing that exalteth itself against the knowledge of God, and bring into captivity every thought to the obedience of Christ.* Too often we try to fight spiritual battles in the flesh throwing insults in response to insults.

6 *And having in a readiness to revenge all disobedience, when your obedience is fulfilled. is Christ's, even so are we Christ's*
7 *Do ye look on things after the outward appearance? If any man trust to himself that he is Christ's, let him of himself think this again, that, as he is Christ's, even so are we Christ's.*

8 *For though I should boast somewhat more of our authority, which the Lord hath given us for edification, and not for your destruction, I should not be ashamed: Remember the authority we have in Christ and learn to use it to defeat the enemy. 2Cor.10:2-8.*

A word about spiritual warfare: many don't realize evil spirits are operating everyday in the lives of millions of people Christians and unbelievers. Just read or watch the news and observe the evil spirits at work; and this doesn't mean a person is possessed by a spirit, just tempted or oppressed. Satan is hard at work on our souls to impede our spiritual growth thus affecting our witness in the world, the task each of us is charged with. The one thing Satan cannot do is cause us to lose our salvation. The book of Job gives us ample lessons:

[1]*There was a man in the land of Uz, whose name was Job; and that man was perfect and upright, and one that feared God, and eschewed evil.* God, Himself, called Job perfect, so also He calls us, the Church, righteous and holy.

[6] *Now there was a day when the sons of God came to present themselves before the LORD, and Satan came also among them.*

[7] *And the LORD said unto Satan, Whence comest thou? Then Satan answered the LORD, and said, From going to and fro in the earth, and from walking up and down in it.*

[8] *And the LORD said unto Satan, Hast thou considered my servant Job, that there is none like him in the earth, a perfect and an upright man, one that feareth God, and escheweth evil?* Satan will come against all of us from time to time.

[9] *Then Satan answered the LORD, and said, Doth Job fear God for nought?*

[10] *Hast not thou made an hedge about him, and about his house, and about all that he hath on every side? thou hast*

blessed the work of his hands, and his substance is increased in the land.

[11] *But put forth thine hand now, and touch all that he hath, and he will curse thee to thy face.*

[12] *And the LORD said unto Satan, Behold, all that he hath is in thy power; only upon himself put not forth thine hand. So Satan went forth from the presence of the LORD.* Job 1:1; 6-12. The Lord has put boundaries on Satan in which he may touch our bodies, wealth, health, but he cannot harm our souls.

Notice: vs.1 states that God himself called Job righteous. The New Testament calls believers *the righteousness of God in Christ Jesus*

For He hath made him to be *sin for us, who knew no sin; that we might be made the righteousness of God in him.* 2Cor.5:21.

As in Job's case Satan could only tempt and torment him because God had already declared him righteous, but Satan was forbidden or barred from destroying Job. Likewise, we who are in Christ are the righteousness of God in Christ. Therefore Satan's only authority is to tempt and torment us through the activities of his fallen angels. This passage lets us know we need to fight our battles with the spiritual weapons divinely given us which gives us authorization to wage war against the enemy in the realm of the spirit not flesh and blood as we're so accustomed to.

Against the Christian are many <u>spirits</u> seeking to work havoc on the Church in general, both corporately as well as the individual. Discernment is vital even though their wake of destruction is evident it may or not mean possession. It may mean oppression.

- There are lying spirits which obviously spread lies both about individuals and the church collectively.
- Spirits of low self esteem causing depression and self destructive thoughts effecting and infecting our health. Strongly suggesting how we were raised, either a positive or negative environment. Low self esteem wars against the natural view of us as a positive, productive citizen.
- Spirit of depression or heaviness…obviously causing depression thus stealing the joy and happiness.
- Spirits of division seeking to cause division in the corporate church as well as the family unit.
- Spirits of pornography or perversion which seek to poison the minds of unsuspecting men and women in the sexual arena.
- Spirits of infirmity which attack the body with sickness and disease.
- Unclean spirits which are unclean in outward appearance revealing the filthiness of the heart.
- There are bullying spirits, hell bent on having their own way in spite of others.
- Unbelieving spirits which cause believers to doubt their faith.

- Spirit of anger. Violence and profanity are often signs of an angry spirit.
- Spirit of jealousy. Envious of anyone for anything and any reason.
- Rebellious spirits which rebel at authority.
- Lying spirits of which need no explanation.

Note: just because a person lies does not mean a lying spirit the person is possessed. Nor are we to brand a person a liar because they told a lie. It may be a part of the individual's weakness he not as yet surrendered to Christ. The same goes with sickness, or disease it may simply be a matter of poor hygiene or a common sickness being transmitted and not a spirit of infirmity and with all the other spirits. A recurring sin on the part of the Christian is due to the old sin nature we carry until the day we're taken home to be with Jesus. It does not mean we're not saved or have never been saved---but simply the old nature is tempting us through Satan. Several passages give us hope and strength: 2Corinthians 10:4-5; James 4:7; 1Pete r5:8-9 and others.

All of which means spirits must be discerned by one who has the gift of discerning of spirits. Much harm can and has been done by such well meaning saints operating in a gift that has not been given them. Many times God's people are so busy "casting out demons" that have no part in the battle. For the Christian <u>cannot be possessed</u>, but most certainly be <u>oppressed</u> by evil spirits.

Simply stated; we live in a world cursed by sickness and disease and harmful emotions that are not necessarily caused by evil spirits.

Jesus warned about evil spirits when He said:

43 *When the unclean spirit is gone out of a man, he walketh through dry places, seeking rest, and findeth none.*

44 *Then he saith, I will return into my house from whence I came out; and when he is come, he findeth it empty, swept, and garnished.*

45 *Then goeth he, and taketh with himself seven other spirits more wicked than himself, and they enter in and dwell there: and the last state of that man is worse than the first. Even so shall it be also unto this wicked generation.* Matt.12:43-45 It takes spiritual discernment to discover these evil spirits and deal with them appropriately. Unfortunately few in the church are skilled in this type of warfare.

Speak to the mountain

Mark 11: 22-24 implores that we should speak to our mountain commanding it to move. When depression comes, it's trying to rape you of your sanity! We are given a sound mind, the mind of Christ. So don't allow the spirit of heaviness rip your spiritual armor off, leaving you naked!

- Shout at that devil don't allow it to rape you of your sanity!
- Enlist other saints to pray for you. It's called intercessory prayer whereas others join you in your personal battles and struggles of life to encourage, strengthen, uplift, pray. Admonish and hold up your weary hands toward heaven to secure your victory. Many times it will be an extended,

prolonged battle, enough to weaken you, if possible, but it will be worth it in the sometimes verrry loooong run!

- Remember, not all saints are aware or of even trained in the use spiritual armor or how to use it, so carefully enlist those who know how. Read David's fight with Goliath 1Samuel 17:1-58.
- Depression leaves in its wake destruction, loss of sanity, health and mental issues, family and friends, children are also affected.
- Worse many come under attack simply because you have been "defeated" [speaking particularly your children it's called "a generational curse"].
- Never play with the devil. Take control of him and yourself in Jesus' name!

Remember, our Heavenly Father leaves nothing to chance.

When the Church collectively and individually neglects time alone in the Word it leaves all sorts of doors wide open for the penetration of evil spirit activity and we have enough to deal with those same spirits in the world, neighbors, workplace etcetera without our families and place of worship.

So often someone is needed to stay and hold up the hands of those in battle until the war is over and victory is manifest.

[10] *So Joshua did what Moses had commanded and fought the army of Amalek. Meanwhile, Moses, Aaron, and Hur climbed to the top of a nearby hill.*

[11] *As long as Moses held up the staff in his hand, the Israelites had the advantage. But whenever he dropped his hand, the Amalekites gained the advantage.*

[12] *Moses' arms soon became so tired he could no longer hold them up. So Aaron and Hur found a stone for him to sit on. Then they stood on each side of Moses, holding up his hands. So his hands held steady until sunset.*

[13] *As a result, Joshua overwhelmed the army of Amalek in battle. Ex. 17:10-13* an army is not of one but many. So also, many times people are fighting an army…not just one enemy at a time. Example: sickness so often involves feelings of fear, depression, self destruction, self pity, low self esteem, unworthiness or a host of other enemies.

Final note: Satan can only steal, kill, and destroy. He cannot force you to do something; he can only tempt you and he does not do good---only evil.

A strong person is not the one who doesn't cry. A strong person is the one who is quiet and sheds tears for a moment, and then picks up the sword to fight again.

Chapter 4

Examining Old Testament prayers

Take note of how these prayers conform to the Altar of Incense and Jesus' pattern for prayer.

Genesis 18:1-33 Abraham's prayer for Sodom and Gomorrah

- What elements from Jesus' pattern for prayer in Matthew 6:9-15 do you observe in Abraham's prayer?
- What things did Jesus instruct the disciples to disregard in Matthew 6:1-8?
- Do you see Abraham disregarding them?
- Were there any negative elements in his prayer? If so, list them.

Numbers 12:1-16 Moses' prayer for Miriam

- What was her sin?
- Why did God inflict her?
- Was her affliction arbitrary or was there a purpose?
- What ingredients do you see in Moses' prayer?
- Was her affliction a mere "zit" or something more serious?

How do these prayers conform or not conform to Jesus' pattern

2 Kings 20: 1-11 Hezekiah's prayer…sickness unto death

1 *In those days was Hezekiah sick unto death. And the prophet Isaiah the son of Amoz came to him, and said unto him, Thus saith the LORD, Set thine house in order; for thou shalt die, and not live.*

2 *Then he turned his face to the wall, and prayed unto the LORD, saying,*

3 *I beseech thee, O LORD, remember now how I have walked before thee in truth and with a perfect heart, and have done that which is good in thy sight. And Hezekiah wept sore.*

4 *And it came to pass, afore Isaiah was gone out into the middle court, that the word of the LORD came to him, saying,*

5 *Turn again, and tell Hezekiah the captain of my people, Thus saith the LORD, the God of David thy father, I have heard thy prayer, I have seen thy tears: behold, I will heal thee: on the third day thou shalt go up unto the house of the LORD.*

6 *And I will add unto thy days fifteen years; and I will deliver thee and this city out of the hand of the king of Assyria; and I will defend this city for mine own sake, and for my servant David's sake.*

7 *And Isaiah said, Take a lump of figs. And they took and laid it on the boil, and he recovered.*

[8] *And Hezekiah said unto Isaiah, What shall be the sign that the LORD will heal me, and that I shall go up into the house of the LORD the third day?*

[9] *And Isaiah said, This sign shalt thou have of the LORD, that the LORD will do the thing that he hath spoken: shall the shadow go forward ten degrees, or go back ten degrees?*

[10] *And Hezekiah answered, It is a light thing for the shadow to go down ten degrees: nay, but let the shadow return backward ten degrees.*

[11] *And Isaiah the prophet cried unto the LORD: and he brought the shadow ten degrees backward, by which it had gone down in the dial of Ahaz.*

Hezekiah had a sickness…unto death, according to the prophet Amos…and pleads with God to spare his life. He then begins his prayer verse 2.

He cites his: life of living righteously before the Lord doing good in truth and a perfect heart and wept sorely [from the very depths of his heart][he cried his eyes out].

Calling on the Lord's record of his life, not his own record, it's a prayer of honesty, humility, integrity, and a lifelong desire to serve the Lord and thus showing adoration and worship. The entire prayer, though very short, is very powerful.

The end result is the Lord heard his cry and added 15 years to his life sending a sign sending the shadow backward ten degrees.

Verse 7 shows a unique method for healing as the prophet places a lump of figs on the boil and Hezekiah recovers. It's important to be led by the Lord in the method used as every malady is to be treated uniquely different. Jesus' examples of healing and prayers are entirely different and unique, demonstrating that every issue must be adhered to by listening to the Spirit.

Hannah's prayer…a closed womb

1Samuel 1:1-28 Hannah wept and prayed for a son promising to dedicate him to the Lord as soon as he was weaned. To be barren in those days was considered a curse, but the Lord had closed her womb. As she wept and prayed Eli, the priest saw her and supposed her to be drunken and tried to chastise her as her lips moved but there was no voice. She replied that she was of a sorrowful spirit and not drunken as supposed. The Lord heard the cries of her heart and she gave birth to Samuel, one of the most profound prophets.

This lesson teaches it's not the exact words we utter that causes God to hear but the brokenness or our hearts. Psalm 34:18 *The Lord is nigh unto them that are of a broken heart; and saveth such as be of a contrite heart.*; Psalm 51: 17 *The sacrifices of God are a broken spirit: a broken and a contrite heart, O God thou wilt not despise.*

Hannah pled her cause albeit with a closed voice out of her sorrow and the Lord heard her.

Unwise prayers

Numbers 11:5 *We remember the fish, which we did eat in Egypt freely; and the cucumbers, and the melons, and the onions, and the garlic:* Israel's complaining against Moses in not having the amenities of Egyptian bondage.

1Kings 19:4b *It is enough: now O Lord, take away my life;* Elijah's foolish plea after Jezebel put a contract on his head.

Jonah 4:3 *Therefore now, O Lord, take, I beseech thee, my life from me; for it is better for me to die than to live.* Jonah's unwise prayer to die after Nineveh's repentance.

Matthew 20:21 *And He said unto her, What wilt thou? She saith unto Him, Grant that these my two sons may sit, the one on thy right hand, and the other on the left, in thy kingdom.* A woman's foolish plea for her sons to be seated in high places in the kingdom.

Thus saith the Lord unto you, Be not afraid nor dismayed by reason of this great multitude; for the battle is not yours, but God's. 2Chron.20:15b.

Chapter 5

Examining New Testament Prayers

How do these prayers compare with Moses' Altar of Incense and Jesus' pattern?

Paul praying for believers:

Ephesians1; Philippians1; Colossians1 and 2Thessalonians1.

- How did Paul address the churches…with love; condemnation, bitterness etcetera?
- Did he admonish the churches?
- If so, in what ways?

Believers praying for one another

2Corinthians 1:11; 2Corinthians 9:14 and Philippians 1:4 shows how Paul prayed for the churches.

- What stands out in these prayers positive or negative?
- Do you see elements of Jesus' pattern for prayer?
- Discuss them.

Mental assent or believing

Mental assenters: those who agree the Bible is true but never act on it. Their decision is one of not obeying that which they "believe".

Believer: one who believes the truths of the Bible based on rock solid evidence and makes a decision and obeys or acts on it. True belief leads to obedience.

- Are you a mentalist or a believer?

[8] Come, behold the works of the LORD, what desolations he hath made in the earth. [9] He maketh wars to cease unto the end of the earth; he breaketh the bow, and cutteth the spear in sunder; he burneth the chariot in the fire. Ps.46:8-9

Chapter 6

Examining the Prayers of Jesus

How do Jesus' prayers correlate with Moses' Altar of Incense?

Yes, his miracles were prayers…on behalf of those in need…they were not sinful in nature, nor for His own benefit but for those to whom were recipients. They were also the answer to His Father's bidding John 8:28-29; Matthew 12:50. Compare them with Moses' Altar of Incense.

Child possessed with demonic spirit

Child possessed with evil spirit causing suicidal actions Mark 9:14-29. [Not all sickness or disease is caused by demonic possession. This must needs be discerned and not arbitrarily assumed.]

Turning water into wine John 2:4-11.

Nobleman's son John 4:46-54.

Draught of fishes Luke 5:1-11.

Peter's mother-in-law healed Matthew 8:14-15; Mark, 1:29-31; Luke 4:38-39.

Walking on the sea Matthew 14:25-33; Mark 6:45-51; John 6:14-19.

Obviously these were but a short list of miracles Jesus did as there are many others recorded in Scripture. However it must be pointed out that:

Jesus was in fact the Temple of God and that the Father dwelt in Him making Him one with the Father. John 2:20-22. [The passage is about the Jews misunderstanding that the Temple would be raised in 3 days, not realizing Jesus was speaking of His body as the Temple of God.

Jesus always did exactly what His Father told Him. John 8:28-29; 11:40-42.

As God, Jesus knew of the lad's possession by the demon.

With regards to Jesus' prayers and miracles, do you see the same elements as in Jesus pattern?

Jesus' public prayers

Matthew 11:25-27 *At that time Jesus answered and said, i thank thee, O Father, Lord of heaven and earth, because thou hast hid these things from the wise and prudent, and hast revealed them unto babes.*

[26]*Even so, Father: for so it seemeth good in thy sight.*

[27]*All things are delivered unto me of my Father: and no man knoweth the Son, but the Father; neither knoweth any man the Father, save the Son, and whomsoever the Son will reveal him.*

John 11:41b And Jesus lifted up His eyes, and said, *Father, I thank thee that thou hast heard me.*

John 17:1-26. These words spake Jesus, and lifted up His eyes to heaven, and said, *Father, the hour is come; glorify thy Son, that the Son also may glorify thee.* Jesus prayer before His hour to be crucified was come.

Consider every prayer as a weapon whether a knife, arrow, spear, or sword smiting the Goliaths in your life of sickness, disease, financial, moral, mental, relational, physical, emotional.

- *As long as you're still praying... you haven't given up!*
- *As long as someone is praying for you... don't give up!*
- *If you are interceding for another... don't give up!*
- *Many are fighting multiple giants simultaneously... don't give up*
- *Call on those warriors who will champion your cause... don't give up!*
- *Make sure those who intercede for you truly believe!*

Chapter 7

Cleansing of the Temple

I learned a very profound lesson while watching the Glenn Ford movie *Heaven and a Gun*, whereas Mr. Ford's part as a gunslinger/preacher attempting to unite the cattlemen and sheepherders using a church, Bible and a gun. Near the end of the movie Caroline Jones, playing his former girlfriend, admonished him "it was not a Bible he was carrying, but a .44 and it was impossible to be both a preacher and a gunslinger". He had to choose one or the other. If a preacher he needed to give God a chance. It got me thinking of whether or not some of us are trying to be both a Christian and whatever we were before salvation. A very sobering thought indeed.

The question becomes: Why a chapter on cleansing the Temple in a manual for Prayer Warriors?

Answer: often a person's problems, we are addressing, have to do with their own personal sin which must be purged or cleansed before healing or deliverance can be manifest.sin as in 1Corinthians 11:23-34, the account of the partaking of communion whereas participants are admonished to first examine or judge themselves before partaking of the sacraments else they be overcome with sickness or early demise. For this cause one might be led to question one's integrity in this light before praying for them. See also James 5:14-16.

Another common thought is that "God does not put sickness on a person". True. However Scripture demonstrates that sin places a person in the precarious position of receiving sickness or an early death upon themselves because our Great God is a jealous God and demands His Temple be kept clean and pure Acts 5:1-11 Ananias and his wife Sapphira, they flat out lied to the Holy Ghost, and 1Corinthians 11:23-34.

The Lord has often used my own personal faults [a fault is not a mere zit or mole, but something worthy of judgment, a sin] to begin a thesis. This time He has chosen to teach me, through my own shortcomings, to chronicle the cleansing of the Temple. Sometimes it may be necessary to admonish those to confess their sins to others that they may be healed. Confessing to God is one thing…but to confess to one another is quite another…however we are admonishes to make it right with others before we go to God. However, we often do the exact opposite and suffer the consequences without realizing it. Holiness with God means we must do it His way and NOT ours. 1Corinthians 5:1-13 chronicles the account of one disciplined by the Corinthian Church for fornication, the purpose of which was to first purge the individual with chastisement, by prohibiting him from fellowshipping with the other believers and to deliver him from destruction from Satan. The other reason was to protect the corporate church from becoming leavened with the same sin.

[23] Therefore if thou bring thy gift to the altar, and there rememberest that thy brother hath ought against thee;

[24] Leave there thy gift before the altar, and go thy way; first be reconciled to thy brother, and then come and offer thy gift.

[25] Agree with thine adversary quickly, whiles thou art in the way with him; lest at any time the adversary deliver thee to the judge, and the judge deliver thee to the officer, and thou be cast into prison. Matt.5:23-25.

Revealed to be healed

As Christians we are forgiven and our sine washed Away by the blood of Jesus Christ. We are declared justified and become the righteousness of God.

22 *Even the righteousness of God which is by faith of Jesus Christ unto all and upon all them that believe: for there is no difference:*

23 *For all have sinned, and come short of the glory of God;*

24 *Being justified freely by his grace through the redemption that is in Christ Jesus:*

25 *Whom God hath set forth to be a propitiation through faith in his blood, to declare his righteousness for the remission of sins that are past, through the forbearance of God;* Rom.3:22-25.

[21] *For he hath made him to be sin for us, who knew no sin; that we might be made the righteousness of God in him.* 2Cor.5:21.

[9] *be found in him, not having mine own righteousness, which is of the law, but that which is through the faith of Christ, the righteousness which is of God by faith:* Phil.3:9.

However, although the sins have been forgiven forever the old sinful nature still exists within each of us which must be purged and cleansed daily as we are all tempted to sin daily. It is that nature to sin that enters the Temple at salvation thus in need of falling prostrate before the throne of our hearts. Therefore the Spirit reveals sinful tendencies like lying, lewdness, pride, complaining, prejudice, spite, adultery, fornication, self-serving indulgence, self-pity the list goes on until the day He takes us home. All these things and more must be purged. It's called "old leaven" 1Corinthians 5:6-10.

Dwelling place of God [represents the spirit]

God has always had a Temple, of sorts. Beginning with the Old Testament Tabernacle in the Wilderness Exodus 40:34

One Tabernacle four temples of God

1) Tabernacle in the Wilderness under Moses…needed to be cleansed daily. While not a "temple" yet the Spirit dwelt there 4o years awaiting the Temple Solomon built.
2) Solomon's Temple…needed to be cleansed daily.

3) Jesus was the Temple of God…sinless, no need of cleansing [the Lamb of God underwent several inspections determining His sinless perfection]
4) The contemporary Church individually and collectively…daily cleansing Romans 12:1-3; Colossians 3:1-15.
5) God is the Temple…no cleansing needed Revelation 21:22.

[34]*Then a cloud covered the tent of the congregation, and the glory of the LORD filled the tabernacle.* Ex.40:34.

[11] *And it came to pass, when the priests were come out of the holy place: (for all the priests that were present were sanctified, and did not then wait by course:*
[12] *Also the Levites which were the singers, all of them of Asaph, of Heman, of Jeduthun, with their sons and their brethren, being arrayed in white linen, having cymbals and psalteries and harps, stood at the east end of the altar, and with them an hundred and twenty priests sounding with trumpets:)*

[13] *It came even to pass, as the trumpeters and singers were as one, to make one sound to be heard in praising and thanking the LORD; and when they lifted up their voice with the trumpets and cymbals and instruments of music, and praised the LORD, saying, For he is good; for his mercy endureth for ever: that then the house was filled with a cloud, even the house of the LORD;*

[14] *So that the priests could not stand to minister by reason of the cloud: for the glory of the LORD had filled the house of God.* 2Chron.5:11-14.

[2] *But I have built an house of habitation for thee, and a place for thy dwelling forever.* 2Chron.6:2.

Note: the term *house* denotes a place of habitation, residence or dwelling place.

New Testament temple

[20] *Then said the Jews, Forty and six years was this temple in building, and wilt thou rear it up in three days?*

[21] *But he spake of the temple of his body.*Jn.2:20-21. If you recall Nicodemus' dialogue with Jesus *No man can do these miracles that thou doest, except be with him.* Jn.3:2c. Overtly states that God was dwelling in the temple of Jesus. Therefore we have the Old Testament Tabernacle of Moses and the Temple built by Solomon and the temple of Jesus plus the New Testament, which is our body. Our bodies are to be kept holy and pure through confession and repentance

[16] *Know ye not that ye are the temple of God, and that the Spirit of God dwelleth in you?*

[17] *If any man defile the temple of God, him shall God destroy; for the temple of God is holy, which temple ye are.*

[18] *Let no man deceive himself. If any man among you seemeth to be wise in this world, let him become a fool, that he may be wise.*

[19] *For the wisdom of this world is foolishness with God. For it is written, He taketh the wise in their own craftiness.* 1Cor.3:16-19.

In each of these temples the divine presence of God, the Holy Spirit dwelt therein and it was mandated that the temple be kept clean.

Whenever an idol was brought into the Old Testament Tabernacle or Temple is was crushed and fallen down before the Ark or the Covenant of God.

Dagon: god of the Philistines ½ man and ½ creature [fish] Dag in Hebrew means fish. The Philistine fish god, religions everywhere worship all kinds of gods. Acts 17:22-23 Paul introduced the UNKNOWN GOD to the residents of Athens Greece, they worshipped many gods. [Many gods are borne out of superstition.] 1Samuel 5 is the account of the Philistines taking the Ark of God and placing it in the house of Dagon overnight. The next day finding Dagon smashed and fallen on his face before the Ark of God.

The New Testament is replete with admonitions to keep your temple clean and purged from all manner of sin and idolatry.

Acts 5:1-11 is the story of Ananias and his wife Sapphira who lied to the Holy Ghost and subsequently died for not repenting of their evil, as the result the entire church feared God. Otherwise it is not unfathomable to surmise chaos in the church.

1Corinthians 5:1-13 a brother reportedly commonly known as a fornicator disciplined; Colossians 3:1-17 duty toward self discipline; 1Corinthians 11:23-34 penalty for not judging oneself before communion; James 5:12-16 to list a few passages regarding church discipline. 1Corinthians 5:1-13 admonishes the church to purge the leaven/sin from the church. It is in accordance with the steps for church discipline in Mathew 18:15-20.

Five steps of Church discipline Matthew 18:15-20

- First: one on one vs. 15
- Second: two on one if the person won't hear the first time. Vs. 16.
- Third: if he neglects to hear after the second admonition the matter is to be taken before the church. Vs. 17.
- Fourth: if he neglects to hear the church he/she is to become as a heathen and a publican. Vs.17.
- Fifth: therein the decisions rendered are bound in heaven and earth. Vs. 18.
- For the discipline of elders 1Timothy 5:19-21 is to be followed.

- Note that if the matter is settled at step one or two it is not necessary to proceed, the matter is handled.

Even Jesus asked where His accusers were for He knew it demanded two or three witnesses of which Pilate produced not one.

Hebrews 12:5-15 instructs believers not to despise God's chastening/discipline for it yields the peaceable fruit of righteousness. It's but another way of saying we are being transformed daily by the renewing of our minds. It is perpetual and on going until Christ takes us home.

Blessings or curses

I challenge you to discern the following from the subsequent passages. Remember, though the passages directly refer to Israel as a nation still the church individually or collectively may be suffering the consequences.

- Is it a blessing or a curse
- Is it personal, relational, financial, emotional, incest, fornication, national, lying, unfaithfulness, name the sin or violation.
- If it is a sin or violation of God's word, how can I turn the curse into a blessing? Remember also that some may choose not to change.
- What happens to those who are in denial or choose not to change? Can their giants be defeated?

Deuteronomy 27:11-26

11 *And Moses charged the people the same day, saying,*

[12] *These shall stand upon mount Gerizim to bless the people, when ye are come over Jordan; Simeon, and Levi, and Judah, and Issachar, and Joseph, and Benjamin:*

[13] *And these shall stand upon mount Ebal to curse; Reuben, Gad, and Asher, and Zebulun, Dan, and Naphtali.*

[14] *And the Levites shall speak, and say unto all the men of Israel with a loud voice,*

[15] *Cursed be the man that maketh any graven or molten image, an abomination unto the LORD, the work of the hands of the craftsman, and putteth it in a secret place. And all the people shall answer and say, Amen.*

[16] *Cursed be he that setteth light by his father or his mother. And all the people shall say, Amen.*

[17] *Cursed be he that removeth his neighbour's landmark. And all the people shall say, Amen.*

[18] *Cursed be he that maketh the blind to wander out of the way. And all the people shall say, Amen.*

[19] *Cursed be he that perverteth the judgment of the stranger, fatherless, and widow. And all the people shall say, Amen.*

[20] *Cursed be he that lieth with his father's wife; because he uncovereth his father's skirt. And all the people shall say, Amen.*

[21] *Cursed be he that lieth with any manner of beast. And all the people shall say, Amen.*

[22] Cursed be he that lieth with his sister, the daughter of his father, or the daughter of his mother. And all the people shall say, Amen.

[23] Cursed be he that lieth with his mother in law. And all the people shall say, Amen.

[24] Cursed be he that smiteth his neighbour secretly. And all the people shall say, Amen.

[25] Cursed be he that taketh reward to slay an innocent person. And all the people shall say, Amen.

[26] Cursed be he that confirmeth not all the words of this law to do them. And all the people shall say, Amen.

Deuteronomy 28:1-68

[1] And it shall come to pass, if thou shalt hearken diligently unto the voice of the LORD *thy God, to observe and to do all his commandments which I command thee this day, that the* LORD *thy God will set thee on high above all nations of the earth:*

[2] And all these blessings shall come on thee, and overtake thee, if thou shalt hearken unto the voice of the LORD *thy God.*

[3] Blessed shalt thou be in the city, and blessed shalt thou be in the field.

[4] Blessed shall be the fruit of thy body, and the fruit of thy ground, and the fruit of thy cattle, the increase of thy kine, and the flocks of thy sheep.

[5] Blessed shall be thy basket and thy store.

[6] *Blessed shalt thou be when thou comest in, and blessed shalt thou be when thou goest out.*

[7] *The* LORD *shall cause thine enemies that rise up against thee to be smitten before thy face: they shall come out against thee one way, and flee before thee seven ways.*

[8] *The* LORD *shall command the blessing upon thee in thy storehouses, and in all that thou settest thine hand unto; and he shall bless thee in the land which the* LORD *thy God giveth thee.*

[9] *The* LORD *shall establish thee an holy people unto himself, as he hath sworn unto thee, if thou shalt keep the commandments of the* LORD *thy God, and walk in his ways.*

[10] *And all people of the earth shall see that thou art called by the name of the* LORD*; and they shall be afraid of thee.*

[11] *And the* LORD *shall make thee plenteous in goods, in the fruit of thy body, and in the fruit of thy cattle, and in the fruit of thy ground, in the land which the* LORD *sware unto thy fathers to give thee.*

[12] *The* LORD *shall open unto thee his good treasure, the heaven to give the rain unto thy land in his season, and to bless all the work of thine hand: and thou shalt lend unto many nations, and thou shalt not borrow.*

[13] *And the* LORD *shall make thee the head, and not the tail; and thou shalt be above only, and thou shalt not be beneath; if that thou hearken unto the commandments of the*

LORD thy God, which I command thee this day, to observe and to do them:

[14] *And thou shalt not go aside from any of the words which I command thee this day, to the right hand, or to the left, to go after other gods to serve them.*

[15] *But it shall come to pass, if thou wilt not hearken unto the voice of the LORD thy God, to observe to do all his commandments and his statutes which I command thee this day; that all these curses shall come upon thee, and overtake thee:*

16 *Cursed shalt thou be in the city, and cursed shalt thou be in the field.*

[17] *Cursed shall be thy basket and thy store.*

[18] *Cursed shall be the fruit of thy body, and the fruit of thy land, the increase of thy kine, and the flocks of thy sheep.*

19 *Cursed shalt thou be when thou comest in, and cursed shalt thou be when thou goest out.*

[20] *The LORD shall send upon thee cursing, vexation, and rebuke, in all that thou settest thine hand unto for to do, until thou be destroyed, and until thou perish quickly; because of the wickedness of thy doings, whereby thou hast forsaken me.*

[21] *The LORD shall make the pestilence cleave unto thee, until he have consumed thee from off the land, whither thou goest to possess it.*

[22] *The* LORD *shall smite thee with a consumption, and with a fever, and with an inflammation, and with an extreme burning, and with the sword, and with blasting, and with mildew; and they shall pursue thee until thou perish.*

[23] *And thy heaven that is over thy head shall be brass, and the earth that is under thee shall be iron.*

[24] *The* LORD *shall make the rain of thy land powder and dust: from heaven shall it come down upon thee, until thou be destroyed.*

[25] *The* LORD *shall cause thee to be smitten before thine enemies: thou shalt go out one way against them, and flee seven ways before them: and shalt be removed into all the kingdoms of the earth.*

[26] *And thy carcase shall be meat unto all fowls of the air, and unto the beasts of the earth, and no man shall fray them away.*

[27] *The* LORD *will smite thee with the botch of Egypt, and with the emerods, and with the scab, and with the itch, whereof thou canst not be healed.*

[28] *The* LORD *shall smite thee with madness, and blindness, and astonishment of heart:*

[29] *And thou shalt grope at noonday, as the blind gropeth in darkness, and thou shalt not prosper in thy ways: and thou shalt be only oppressed and spoiled evermore, and no man shall save thee.*

[30] *Thou shalt betroth a wife, and another man shall lie with*
her: thou shalt build an house, and thou shalt not dwell therein:
thou shalt plant a vineyard, and shalt not gather the grapes
thereof.

[31] *Thine ox shall be slain before thine eyes, and thou shalt not*
eat thereof: thine ass shall be violently taken away from before
thy face, and shall not be restored to thee: thy sheep shall be
given unto thine enemies, and thou shalt have none to rescue
them.

[32] *Thy sons and thy daughters shall be given unto another*
people, and thine eyes shall look, and fail with longing for them
all the day long; and there shall be no might in thine hand.

[33] *The fruit of thy land, and all thy labours, shall a nation*
which thou knowest not eat up; and thou shalt be only
oppressed and crushed alway:

[34] *So that thou shalt be mad for the sight of thine eyes which*
thou shalt see.

[35] *The* LORD *shall smite thee in the knees, and in the legs, with*
a sore botch that cannot be healed, from the sole of thy foot unto
the top of thy head.

[36] *The* LORD *shall bring thee, and thy king which thou shalt*
set over thee, unto a nation which neither thou nor thy fathers
have known; and there shalt thou serve other gods, wood and
stone.

[37] *And thou shalt become an astonishment, a proverb, and a byword, among all nations whither the LORD shall lead thee.*

[38] *Thou shalt carry much seed out into the field, and shalt gather but little in; for the locust shall consume it.*

[39] *Thou shalt plant vineyards, and dress them, but shalt neither drink of the wine, nor gather the grapes; for the worms shall eat them.*

[40] *Thou shalt have olive trees throughout all thy coasts, but thou shalt not anoint thyself with the oil; for thine olive shall cast his fruit.*

[41] *Thou shalt beget sons and daughters, but thou shalt not enjoy them; for they shall go into captivity.*

[42] *All thy trees and fruit of thy land shall the locust consume.*

[43] *The stranger that is within thee shall get up above thee very high; and thou shalt come down very low.*

[44] *He shall lend to thee, and thou shalt not lend to him: he shall be the head, and thou shalt be the tail.*

[45] *Moreover all these curses shall come upon thee, and shall pursue thee, and overtake thee, till thou be destroyed; because thou hearkenedst not unto the voice of the LORD thy God, to keep his commandments and his statutes which he commanded thee:*

[46] *And they shall be upon thee for a sign and for a wonder, and upon thy seed for ever.*

[47] *Because thou servedst not the* LORD *thy God with joyfulness, and with gladness of heart, for the abundance of all things;*

[48] *Therefore shalt thou serve thine enemies which the* LORD *shall send against thee, in hunger, and in thirst, and in nakedness, and in want of all things: and he shall put a yoke of iron upon thy neck, until he have destroyed thee.*

[49] *The* LORD *shall bring a nation against thee from far, from the end of the earth, as swift as the eagle flieth; a nation whose tongue thou shalt not understand;*

[50] *A nation of fierce countenance, which shall not regard the person of the old, nor shew favour to the young:*

[51] *And he shall eat the fruit of thy cattle, and the fruit of thy land, until thou be destroyed: which also shall not leave thee either corn, wine, or oil, or the increase of thy kine, or flocks of thy sheep, until he have destroyed thee.*

[52] *And he shall besiege thee in all thy gates, until thy high and fenced walls come down, wherein thou trustedst, throughout all thy land: and he shall besiege thee in all thy gates throughout all thy land, which the* LORD *thy God hath given thee.*

[53] *And thou shalt eat the fruit of thine own body, the flesh of thy sons and of thy daughters, which the* LORD *thy God hath given thee, in the siege, and in the straitness, wherewith thine enemies shall distress thee:*

[54] *So that the man that is tender among you, and very delicate, his eye shall be evil toward his brother, and toward the wife of*

his bosom, and toward the remnant of his children which he shall leave:

55 *So that he will not give to any of them of the flesh of his children whom he shall eat: because he hath nothing left him in the siege, and in the straitness, wherewith thine enemies shall distress thee in all thy gates.*

56 *The tender and delicate woman among you, which would not adventure to set the sole of her foot upon the ground for delicateness and tenderness, her eye shall be evil toward the husband of her bosom, and toward her son, and toward her daughter,*

57 *And toward her young one that cometh out from between her feet, and toward her children which she shall bear: for she shall eat them for want of all things secretly in the siege and straitness, wherewith thine enemy*

58 *If thou wilt not observe to do all the words of this law that are written in this book, that thou mayest fear this glorious and fearful name,* THE LORD THY GOD;

59 *Then the* LORD *will make thy plagues wonderful, and the plagues of thy seed, even great plagues, and of long continuance, and sore sicknesses, and of long continuance.*

60 *Moreover he will bring upon thee all the diseases of Egypt, which thou wast afraid of; and they shall cleave unto thee.*

61 *Also every sickness, and every plague, which is not written in the book of this law, them will the* LORD *bring upon thee,*

until thou be destroyed.

62 *And ye shall be left few in number, whereas ye were as the stars of heaven for multitude; because thou wouldest not obey the voice of the LORD thy God.*

63 *And it shall come to pass, that as the LORD rejoiced over you to do you good, and to multiply you; so the LORD will rejoice over you to destroy you, and to bring you to nought; and ye shall be plucked from off the land whither thou goest to possess it.*

64 *And the LORD shall scatter thee among all people, from the one end of the earth even unto the other; and there thou shalt serve other gods, which neither thou nor thy fathers have known, even wood and stone.*

65 *And among these nations shalt thou find no ease, neither shall the sole of thy foot have rest: but the LORD shall give thee there a trembling heart, and failing of eyes, and sorrow of mind:*

66 *And thy life shall hang in doubt before thee; and thou shalt fear day and night, and shalt have none assurance of thy life:*

67 *In the morning thou shalt say, Would God it were even! and at even thou shalt say, Would God it were morning! for the fear of thine heart wherewith thou shalt fear, and for the sight of thine eyes which thou shalt see.*

68 *And the LORD shall bring thee into Egypt again with ships, by the way whereof I spake unto thee, Thou shalt see it no more again: and there ye shall be sold unto your enemies for bondmen and bondwomen, and no man shall buy you.*

To summarize: as *Goliath Slayers* we may be called upon to admonish one to confess their sins to cleanse their Temple that they might be healed. Disobedience produces curses or giants in our lives and must be dealt with to turn the curses into blessings. The preceding passages happened to Israel either because of obedience or disobedience to God's word and, unfortunately, it is happening in the church today.

[6] Blessed are they which do hunger and thirst after righteousness: for they shall be filled. Matt. 5:6

Chapter 8

Laying on of Hands

The Laying on of Hands is quite often misunderstood or taken for granted when in fact it represents a very solemn occasion. Our Great and Mighty, Awesome God still and always has been Holy…separate from sin and therefore demands the ultimate in respect.

Definition: the action of a spiritual blessing or curse flowing or being transferred from one person to another, the act of touching: [30]*And Jesus, immediately knowing in Himself that virtue had gone out of Him, turned about in the press of the crowd and said, "Who touched My clothes?* Mk.5:30. This is primarily intended for the use of those in the presbytery however, anyone, especially with the gift of healing may lay hands on a person when under the anointing to do so.

Examples

- Aaron and Hur lifting up Moses hands for Israel's victory over Amalek in Rephidim Exodus 17:10-12.
- Aaron laying hands on goat with sins to be sent into the wilderness Leviticus 16:18-21…a pre-incarnate depiction of Christ's trial.

laying hands on the head for healing, blessing, introduced into a position of authority or any other possibilities.

- Laying hands on sick child.
- Woman with issue of blood touching the hem of Jesus' garment Mark 15:21-34. (She initiated the touch).

[21]*And Aaron shall lay both his hands upon the head of the live goat, and confess over him all the iniquities of the children of Israel, and all their transgressions in all their sins, putting them upon the head of the goat, and shall send him away by the hand of a fit man into the wilderness:* Lev.16:21.

The transference of sins of the people to the scapegoat, Jesus became our scapegoat when those prosecuting Him took Him, beat Him, and crucified Him.

[54]*And it was so, that when Solomon had made an end of praying all this prayer and supplication unto the LORD, he arose from the altar of the LORD, from kneeling on his knees with his hands spread up to heaven.* 1Ki.8:54. This is the reverse act of reaching toward heaven to receive the blessing instead of the person laying their hands upon someone. Reaching toward heaven is also a form of worship without expectation of a blessing.

Pronouncing a blessing lifting hands toward a people

[22]*And Aaron lifted up his hand toward the people, and blessed them, and came down from offering of the sin offering, and the burnt offering, and peace offerings.* Lev.9:22. Lifting hands toward the people and pronounced a blessing.

Lifting hands without touching

[50] *And he led them out as far as to Bethany, and he lifted up his hands, and blessed them.* Lu.24:50. Jesus lifted His hands without touching them.

Laying on of Hands for another, proxy

It's called proxy for when a person stands in the stead of another in their absence. This may happen more often than we realize, but prayer is often the intercession for another and quite often includes the Laying on of Hands. No matter the geographical location or distance.

Jacob blessing and cursing his twelve sons

[1] *And Jacob called unto his sons, and said, Gather yourselves together, that I may tell you that which shall befall you* in the last days.

[2] *Gather yourselves together, and hear, ye sons of Jacob; and hearken unto Israel your father.*

[3] *Reuben, thou art my firstborn, my might, and the beginning of my strength, the Excellency of dignity, and the Excellency of power:*

[4] *Unstable as water, thou shalt not excel; because thou wentest up to thy father's bed; then defiledst thou it: he went up to my couch.* Curse pronounced.

[5] *Simeon and Levi are brethren; instruments of cruelty are in their habitations.*

[6] *O my soul, come not thou into their secret; unto their assembly, mine honour, be not thou united: for in their anger they slew a man, and in their selfwill they digged down a wall.*

[7] *Cursed be their anger, for it was fierce; and their wrath, for it was cruel: I will divide them in Jacob, and scatter them in Israel.* Curse pronounced.

[8] *Judah, thou art he whom thy brethren shall praise: thy hand shall be in the neck of thine enemies; thy father's children shall bow down before thee.*

[9] *Judah is a lion's whelp: from the prey, my son, thou art gone up: he stooped down, he couched as a lion, and as an old lion; who shall rouse him up?*

[10] *The sceptre shall not depart from Judah, nor a lawgiver from between his feet, until Shiloh come; and unto him shall the gathering of the people be.*

[11] *Binding his foal unto the vine, and his ass's colt unto the choice vine; he washed his garments in wine, and his clothes in the blood of grapes:*

[12] *His eyes shall be red with wine, and his teeth white with milk.* Blessing pronounced.

[13] *Zebulun shall dwell at the haven of the sea; and he shall be for an haven of ships; and his border shall be unto Zidon.* Blessing pronounced.

[14] *Issachar is a strong ass couching down between two burdens:*

[15] *And he saw that rest was good, and the land that it was pleasant; and bowed his shoulder to bear, and became a servant unto tribute.* Blessing pronounced.

[16] *Dan shall judge his people, as one of the tribes of Israel.* Blessing pronounced.

[17] *Dan shall be a serpent by the way, an adder in the path, that biteth the horse's heels, so that his rider shall fall backward.* Curse pronounced.

[18] *I have waited for thy salvation, O LORD.* Curse pronounced.

[19] *Gad, a troop shall overcome him: but he shall overcome at the last.*

[20] *Out of Asher his bread shall be fat, and he shall yield royal dainties.*

[21] *Naphtali is a hind let loose: he giveth goodly words.*

[22] *Joseph is a fruitful bough, even a fruitful bough by a well; whose branches run over the wall:*

[23] *The archers have sorely grieved him, and shot at him, and hated him:*

[24] *But his bow abode in strength, and the arms of his hands were made strong by the hands of the mighty God of Jacob; (from thence is the shepherd, the stone of Israel:)*

[25] *Even by the God of thy father, who shall help thee; and by the Almighty, who shall bless thee with blessings of heaven above, blessings of the deep that lieth under, blessings of the breasts, and of the womb:*

[26] *The blessings of thy father have prevailed above the blessings of my progenitors unto the utmost bound of the everlasting hills: they shall be on the head of Joseph, and on the*

crown of the head of him that was separate from his brethren. Blessing pronounced.

[27] *Benjamin shall ravin as a wolf: in the morning he shall devour the prey, and at night he shall divide the spoil.*

This passage demonstrates the necessity of a father's blessing, [it is the father who pronounces the blessing or curse] however it must be based on the unction [moving or anointing] of the Father in heaven and not simply our fleshly appetites. Jacob knew his sons well enough to know whether they would love the Lord or not. Their blessing or curse was pronounced accordingly.

Joseph lays hands on Ephraim and Manasseh

[13] *And Joseph took them both, Ephraim in his right hand toward Israel's left hand, and Manasseh in his left hand toward Israel's right hand, and brought them near unto him.*

[14] *And Israel stretched out his right hand, and laid it upon Ephraim's head, who was the younger, and his left hand upon Manasseh's head, guiding his hands wittingly; for Manasseh was the firstborn.* The younger, Ephraim, received the *birthright* in the stead of Manasseh, the eldest or firstborn.

[15] *And he blessed Joseph, and said, God, before whom my fathers Abraham and Isaac did walk, the God which fed me all my life long unto this day,*

[16] *The Angel which redeemed me from all evil, bless the lads; and let my name be named on them, and the name of my*

fathers Abraham and Isaac; and let them grow into a multitude in the midst of the earth.

[17] *And when Joseph saw that his father laid his right hand upon the head of Ephraim, it displeased him: and he held up his father's hand, to remove it from Ephraim's head unto Manasseh's head.*

[18] *And Joseph said unto his father, Not so, my father: for this is the firstborn; put thy right hand upon his head.* The only reason for the switch appears to be divine prophecy not a random choice.

[20] *And he blessed them that day, saying, In thee shall Israel bless, saying, God make thee as Ephraim and as Manasseh: and he set Ephraim before Manasseh.* Gen.48.13-20. Joseph laid his hands upon his son Ephraim with his right hand, a symbol of power and authority although he was the younger of the two…this was a divine prophecy that the younger should have the *birthright* as opposed to the eldest. Also demonstrating the soberness of laying on of hands. It ought not to be taken lightly for it has divine authority behind it.

Notice: that each blessing or curse pronounced had a definitive divine reason they are divine pronouncements of the Spirit not the flesh.

Admonition against hastily laying on of hands

[22] *Lay hands suddenly on no man, neither be partaker of other men's sins: keep thyself pure.* 1Tim.5:22. Paul warned Timothy not to be hasty in laying hands on a person either for ordination or restoration of a backslider.

Such delicate matters must be under divine guidance, even for healing.

Blessing on children

Recently my son asked for me to write a blessing for his three young boys ages 4 ½, 1 ½ and 7 months. Realizing the tremendous task which I'd been requested I immediately prayed about the matter for several weeks, originally asking for a separate blessing for each, then the Lord gave me one blessing for all three. Further realizing now I needed to lay hands on them, so one evening I gathered them all into my lap, anointed each with oil and read the blessing with their proud parents looking on. What a blessing, privilege and enormous task it was. But all joy! As you can see laying hands on someone and praying a blessing on them is an awesome responsibility for who can predict the future of another without divine guidance?

Stir up the gift

[6] *Wherefore I put thee in remembrance that thou stir up the gift of God, which is in thee by the putting on of my hands.* We are to stir up or practice the gifts endued upon us by the laying on of hands.

[7] *For God hath not given us the spirit of fear; but of power, and of love, and of a sound mind.* 2Tim.1:6-7. Sometimes we can become fearful concerning spiritual matters, but *God has not given us the spirit of fear.* Operate in your spiritual gifts under divine guidance. Ultimately it means we have to learn to hear the voice of God and then we need to learn to obey His voice, entirely two different things.

Indeed many other methods of Laying on of Hands are manifest but only a few are depicted herein.

Surround yourself with God's Word.

Chapter 9

Hearing God's Voice

Vital to ministry

By far the most vital part of any sphere of ministry is that of hearing God's voice. Hearing His voice is most precious…obeying His voice is of utmost importance. Without hearing God's voice be it the Pastorate, deacon, elder, in prayer or anywhere else one is doomed to frustration and failure.

Personally I was brought up with a Baptist background whereas hearing God's was never brought up or taught. Later after I got "sure enough saved", as taught in some Pentecostal circles, it was encouraged to "follow your Holy Ghost"…without a trace of training/teaching. From time to time I personally heard God's voice, though not audible, but always with training. And still I continued to seek out His voice for myself. Even in Bible College it was not taught in fact we were taught that the last time God spoke was through His Son Jesus Christ Hebrews 1:1-2. No other religion hears his/her god's voice…only the Christian.

[11] *Now there dwelt an old prophet in Bethel; and his sons came and told him all the works that the man of God had done that day in Bethel: the words which he had spoken unto the king, them they told also to their father.*

[12] *And their father said unto them, What way went he? For his sons had seen what way the man of God went, which came from Judah.*

[13] *And he said unto his sons, Saddle me the ass. So they saddled him the ass: and he rode thereon,*

[14] *And went after the man of God, and found him sitting under an oak: and he said unto him, Art thou the man of God that camest from Judah? And he said, I am.*

[15] *Then he said unto him, Come home with me, and eat bread.*

[16] *And he said, I may not return with thee, nor go in with thee: neither will I eat bread nor drink water with thee in this place:*

[17] *For it was said to me by the word of the LORD, Thou shalt eat no bread nor drink water there, nor turn again to go by the way that thou camest.*

[18] *He said unto him, I am a prophet also as thou art; and an angel spake unto me by the word of the LORD, saying, Bring him back with thee into thine house, that he may eat bread and drink water. But he lied unto him.*

[19] *So he went back with him, and did eat bread in his house, and drank water.*

[20] *And it came to pass, as they sat at the table, that the word of the LORD came unto the prophet that brought him back:*

[21] *And he cried unto the man of God that came from Judah, saying, Thus saith the LORD, Forasmuch as thou hast disobeyed the mouth of the LORD, and hast not kept the commandment which the LORD thy God commanded thee,*

[22] *But camest back, and hast eaten bread and drunk water in the place, of the which the Lord did say to thee, Eat no bread, and drink no water; thy carcass shall not come unto the sepulcher of thy fathers.* 1Ki.13:11-22. This passage illustrates both the importance of hearing and discerning God's voice and also obeying His voice.

Except the Lord build the house

[1]*Except the LORD build the house, they labour in vain that build it: except the LORD keep the city, the watchman waketh but in vain.* Ps.127:1. To me this illustrates that if one does not hear God's voice whatever they are attempting to build is in vain…no matter how huge! It matters not if it's a church with a pastor, a prayer ministry or whatever. You must hear God's voice and leading.

[1]*Verily, verily, I say unto you, He that entereth not by the door into the sheepfold, but climbeth up some other way, the same is a thief and a robber.*

[2] *But he that entereth in by the door is the shepherd of the sheep.*

[3] *To him the porter openeth; and the sheep hear his voice: and*
he calleth his own sheep by name, and leadeth them out.

[4] *And when he putteth forth his own sheep, he goeth before*
them, and the sheep follow him: for they know his voice.

[5] *And a stranger will they not follow, but will flee from him: for*
they know not the voice of strangers. Jn.10:1-5.

Patricharchs

Genesis 2-3; Adam walked and conversed with God before the fall

Genesis 4:6-15 God's dialogue with Cain

Genesis 5: 22 Enoch walked with God (shows relationship)

Genesis 6-9 God's relationship and dialogue with Noah

Genesis 12-50_God's relationship and dialogue with Abram/Abraham and his posterity

Exodus 3:1-22 God's dialogue with Moses

Numbers 22:22-35 God speaks to Balaam's ass/donkey then to Balaam

1Kings 19:4-18 the Lord speaks to Elijah the prophet in a <u>still small voice</u>

Psalms 46:10 It's impossible to hear God voice without being still.

Acts 9: 1-9 Saul's encounter with Jesus on the road to Damascus

2 Peter 1:20-21 God spoke as they were moved by the Holy Ghost

[1] *Verily, verily, I say unto you, He that entereth not by the door into the sheepfold, but climbeth up some other way, the same is a thief and a robber.*

[2]*But he that entereth in by the door is the shepherd of the sheep.*

[3]*To him the porter openeth; and the sheep hear his voice: and he calleth his own sheep by name, and leadeth them out.*

[4]*And when he putteth forth his own sheep, he goeth before them, and the sheep follow him: for they know his voice.*

[5]*And a stranger will they not follow, but will flee from him: for they know not the voice of strangers.* Jn. 10:1-5.

Its often been said that "God moves in mysterious ways", however, that's incorrect as history shows that God always lets His people know what he's going to do long before He actually does it---it's called prophecy. Even so God's ways may seem mysterious to unbelievers as well to the unlearned believers.

Surely the Lord GOD will do nothing, but he revealeth his secret unto his servants the prophets. Am.3:7. A secret is something kept hidden. There are many "secrets" revealed in this book that many have not taken the time and effort to discover through study of God's Word. The Chapter on Heaven in *Understanding the Christian Birthright* is but one example for there are many things about heaven I did not know until I studied heaven, it was revealed to me. Now they are no longer secrets to me for God revealed them through the study of His Word.

Just read the prophecies concerning the Messiah's birth, death, burial and resurrection. That's proof positive that God always lets His people know aforetime.

- Adam heard Him in the garden Genesis 2-3.
- Abram heard Him call him out of Haran Genesis 12:1-9 advising him of the future as a great man, the father of Israel and multitudes.
- Noah, Enoch, Moses, Joseph, Daniel, David, Samuel, the prophets, apostles, disciples, Mary the mother of Jesus, Joseph his stepfather, on and on and on we are told of those who heard God's voice and received instructions to obey.
- Even newborn babies learn to hear the voices of their parents. It is their *birthright.*
- Why shouldn't we learn his voice as well? It is our *birthright* to hear our Father's voice John 10:1-5.
- No other religion can boast of hearing the voice of their god, read Psalm 115:1-8. [Their gods cannot speak let alone hear, see, touch, feel, love, provide etcetera.]
- I remember the very first time I heard God speak to me was in the summer of 1974 on the loading docks of the Sears store I worked in at that time. He spoke my name as clearly as two people sitting together and gave me instructions to quit my job and start shoeing

horses fulltime. I was startled at first and looked around to see who it was. Then he spoke again and repeated the instructions. Remember when God spoke to Samuel for the first time in 1Samuel 3:4-10, that was me! I had never heard God's voice before. Yet the Lord spoke four times until Samuel finally responded. This was directly opposed to common sense however I obeyed and was blessed! Often times Scripture records God telling someone to do something completely out of sync with reality, but if you come to know His voice, you can obey faithfully..

Note: not everyone hears God exactly the same way, but there are similar methods and ways to hear his voice.

- Balaam heard God's voice through a dumb ass [many say donkey, KJV says ass] which crushed his foot against a rock to get his attention *And the LORD opened the mouth of the ass, and she said unto Balaam, What have I done unto thee, that thou hast smitten me these three times?* Num.22:28.
- Written Word Hebrews 8:10-11.
- Dreams and visions Acts 2:17.
- Open vision John 1:18, Jesus saw Nathanael under the fig tree, before He met him.
- Audible voice Mark 1:11 the voice from heaven declaring Jesus as the Son of God. Acts 9:3-6 Saul heard the voice of Jesus and was blinded. [It must be noted that only Saul heard the voice of God, no one else in his party heard the voice.]
- Still small voice 1Kings 19:11-13.

- Godly counsel Proverbs 11:14.
- Prophetic Word 2 Peter 1:20-21.
- Two or three witnesses or confirmation Matthew 18: 15-18 [church discipline].
- Life's circumstances Acts 18:1-3.
- The peace of God which passes understanding Philippians 4:7.

The Guidelines

1. The voice you hear must not and will not violate or run amiss of sound theology and hermeneutically correct studies/teachings. While the specifics are not usually found "written in the Word" yet the principles are and must always be fully supported by the written word by precept and example.
2. The message from the voice must and will always come to pass exactly as spoken otherwise it is not from God. This is called prophecy. A prophet was a seer, one who had divine insight and knowledge.
3. The child of God must, (not an option or hap-hazard); both develop and maintain a deep relationship with the Lord as an on-going daily basis through worship, praise, and study of the WORD as well as reading.
4. If God does not hear from you, how and why should you hear from Him?
5. God's voice will never-ever violate or transgress His written WORD, though at times it may super-cede the laws of nature

and/or human logic (I believe this to be the exception rather than the rule).

6. The voice you hear will never violate God's character.
7. God speaks to enhance our relationship with Him.
8. He always desires our intimacy with Him…that being through His voice.

One mouth two ears

If any of you lack wisdom, let him ask of God, that giveth to all men liberally, and upbraideth not; and it shall be given him. But let him ask in faith, nothing wavering. For he that wavereth is like a wave of the sea driven with the wind and tossed. For let not that man think that he shall receive anything of the Lord. Jas.1:5-7. God has given is two ears to listen to others, and to God. He gave us one mouth was given that we might listen first and speak afterwards.

Note: no one hears God the same way as everyone else, nor does it sound the same, but there are similar methods and ways to hear his voice.

Still small voice

11 *And he said, Go forth, and stand upon the mount before the LORD. And, behold, the LORD passed by, and a great and strong wind rent the mountains, and brake in pieces the rocks before the LORD; but the LORD was not in the wind: and after the wind an earthquake; but the LORD was not in the earthquake:*

[12]*And after the earthquake a fire; but the LORD was not in the fire: and after the fire a still small voice.* There is no explanation of the wind, fire, and earthquake other than it represents our emotional state. God's voice is soft, not loud and boisterous, therefore when our emotions are at a crescendo we need to step aside, pray for peace in our hearts and souls and wait to hear God's voice. It's far too dangerous to act or speak when we're all uptight. Simmer down!

I used to watch the deep sea diving operations on television. The ship might be going through choppy waters but the diver, far below, on the ocean floor, was experiencing utter silence and calm. We need to dive beneath our emotions to the peace of God awaiting us…then we can hear His voice.

[13]*And it was so, when Elijah heard it, that he wrapped his face in his mantle, and went out, and stood in the entering in of the cave. And, behold, there came a voice unto him, and said, What doest thou here, Elijah?* 1Ki.19:11-13. It was not until after the storms in Elijah's life [remember, Jezebel had put out a contract on his life 1Kings 19:1-10, after that he, Elijah had slain the 450 prophets of Baal in 1Kings 18:1-46]. Elijah needed to rest and chill out. He was emotionally distraught. We cannot hear His voice when we are distraught!

Benefits of hearing His voice

- We learn to follow Him John 10:4.
- Psalm 23 says: he provides green pastures [plenty of food natural and spiritual].
- Leads by still waters. Jesus told the Samaritan woman at the well she would never thirst again if we would drink of Him John 4:4-26.

- Restores our souls in stressful times.
- Leads in paths of righteousness. He is with us in times of great sorrow and death.
- Because we are His children He sets our table, provides, in the presence of our enemies.
- Our head is anointed with oil. The anointing and empowerment of the Holy Ghost.
- We have plenty of material goods as well as spiritual.
- Goodness and mercy follow us every day even in rough times.
- The Lord's house may be construed as heaven.
- He gives us wisdom and understanding.
- Hearing God's voice eliminates trial and error, embarrassment, and produces the fruit of His Word. Perhaps the reason prayers aren't answered is because we are praying our will instead of God's will.
- Jesus always prayed and did that which the Father told him…which is why the Pharisees said He taught with authority not as the scribes Mathew 7:29. Many today, call this an anointing. Anointed words carry more weight than ordinary words.

God's people are missing so much by not listening for His voice. Remember He gave the Law of Moses that we might prosper and be successful Joshua 1:6-9.

Common Hindrances

- Lack of training and guidance on hearing God's voice.

- Too much of a hurry.
- Acting on the first "voice" they hear.
- Failure to discern between God's voice and the voice of the flesh. Far too many Christians, myself included, have acted on their fleshly appetites in "doing the work of the Lord" finding themselves out of God's will, yet still unable to acknowledge their mistake/s.
- Failure to confirm the voice. [There are a multitude of voices.]

.[9]*Or what man is there of you, whom if his son ask bread, will he give him a stone?*

[10]*Or if he ask a fish, will he give him a serpent?* Will God give us the opposite of what we ask for?

Beware but not fearful

[1]*Beloved, believe not every spirit, but try the spirits whether they are of God: because many false prophets are gone out into the world.* [2]*Hereby know ye the Spirit of God: Every spirit that confesseth that Jesus Christ is come in the flesh is of God.* [3]*And every spirit that confesseth not that Jesus Christ is come in the flesh is not of God: and this is the spirit of antichrist, whereof ye have heard that it should come; and even now already is it in the world.* 1Jn.4:1-3.

By necessity every Christian needs to *try the spirits whether they are of God.* It behooves each of us to learn God's voice and follow it with great joy. Just because a person is a 'great orator' and knows the Word inside out is no guarantee of the Spirit's leading. Satan has been around since the beginning of time and he knows the Word often quoting it verbatim thus misleading God's people.

Chapter 10

Compassion

Quite often people, not knowing what to expect, will ask a rather generic and vague request such as for their finances or family or employment and such like thus giving the prayer warrior either a choice of uttering an equally vague petition or to ask leading question/s to promote a more accurate petition. For example; the petitioner asks for prayer concerning finances instead of simply praying you might ask for more clarification---Are you having difficulty paying your bills? Or; "Are you looking for employment?" The subsequent questions will secure a more definitive request thus allowing you ample information to more properly pray. However, whenever you're asking questions beware of being too personal and like you're prying into "none of your business" thus offending the very one you're tryiny to help.

Compassion characteristics

- Compassion often requires asking questions and also serves to demonstrate to the petitioner that you, the intercessor, really do care…further demonstrating compassion. Caution: if too many or questions are too personal it could lead to a more intimate relationship between petitioner and prayer warrior thus creating an undesirable bonding. For this reason many churches discourage inter-gender praying…especially for an extended period of time.

- Compassion is not a "quick fix". Some petitioners want you to fix or solve their problems. However, many are reluctant to work on themselves to solve their problems. For example; if a petitioner is in debt due to their personal ineptness in finances but refuses counsel to correct their financial issues then all the prayers you may pronounce will fall on deaf ears and be of no effect to the petitioner. In short many issues require educating one's self and taking proper steps to correct their errors. Praying for relationship issues may require one to take marital or relationship classes.
- Compassion is an expression of love in action.
- Compassion is being a friend to the lonely.
- Compassion does not seek to "solve" all their problems but to meet the immediate needs of comfort, encouragement and many times advice or confession where appropriate.
- Compassion tends to bond the petitioner with the prayer warrior. Thus when asked by an opposite gender for prayer, it's highly advisable to enlist the assistance of a like gender, preferably one's own spouse. Can be formed especially between inter-gender experiences and must be quenched.
- Compassion is not pity or feeling sorry for another.

- Compassion is experiencing the full gamut of emotions as the petitioner.
- Compassion, a noun, is a deep feeling of sympathy [much different than mere pity] which leads to action [verb] see the Good Samaritan Luke 10:30-37. It has the desire to alleviate the pain or remove its cause. Notice the same passage the priest and Levite both witnessed the very same man in dire need but both walked around the situation. Nothing is said of their feelings toward the victim; however it can possibly be a total lack of feeling toward the victim.
- Compassion involves confidentiality and is a must for both parties for to violate confidence undermine the whole integrity of the prayer warrior.
- Compassion may in fact take an extended period of time covering sometimes a multitude of issues the petitioner is facing. The more questions you ask the more issues are revealed and the more time it takes to bring about a suitable level of comfort for the petitioner. It is without this knowledge that the intercessor may become frustrated, sometimes to the point of giving up.
- Compassion is mourning with those that mourn and rejoicing with those that are rejoicing.
- Compassion is the antidote for pain and suffering, without pain and suffering compassion is but a clanging cymbal.
- Therefore revel in God's compassion rather than wallowing in the muck and mire of pain and suffering.

- Faith is built by meditating in the Word of God thus preparing our heart and spirit to receive from Him. It also builds compassion.
- Trying to pray to cause faith to work is futile, it's the reverse. It's our faith that makes prayer work. And our faith comes from hearing God's Word through meditation and preparation of the heart thus our heart hears Romans 10:8-11.
- Faith is a matter of the heart not the recitation of words.
- Praying God's Word is not magical or manipulative and has no set pattern or device with which to accomplish that our petition.
- Authoritative prayers of power stem from the Old Testament pattern of the Altar of Incense and Jesus' empowerment upon believers Matthew 28:18-20; Mark 16:15-20. Only certain ingredients were allowed to be mixed together to present the sweet smelling aroma that ascends to the Throne of God, anything else was and is totally unacceptable. To add anger, malice, vengeance, lust, jealousy or any other sin makes our prayers unacceptable and pungent as opposed to a sweet smelling aroma, Exodus 30:9; Isaiah 58:3-12; Revelation 5:8.

Scriptures to remind us to speak words of encouragement

A wholesome tongue is a tree of life. Pr. 15:4

Pleasant words are as an honeycomb, sweet to the soul, and health to the bones. Pr.16:24

Death and life are in the power of the tongue: and they love it shall eat the fruit thereof. Pr.18:21.

A word fitly spoken is like apples of gold in pictures of silver. As an earring of gold, and an ornament of fine gold, so is a wise reprove upon an obedient ear. Pr.25:11-12

Chapter 11

Pray the Word

Praying the Word, not mere recitation, is powerful for it reveals God's will for our lives. We are literally praying God's will for our lives and for those we are interceding for. Therefore if we want power in our prayers we must pray the Word. Then we will be confidant knowing that He hears us. Prayer is powerful because it is HOLY…ordained of God. Praying the Word is praying God's will for our lives. We ought not to take prayer for granted…it is HOLY. We ought not to disrespect prayer with childish mutterings which must be done away with as we mature in Christ.

[14] *And this is the confidence that we have in him, that, if we ask any thing according to his will, he heareth us:*

[15] *And if we know that he hear us, whatsoever we ask, we know that we have the petitions that we desired of him. 1John 5:14-15.*

Save your vocal cords

Praying for power does not mean we need to raises our voices or scream and shout to make ourselves heard. It means praying God's Word in every situation---therein is the power! The more I read of Jesus prayers the more I'm convinced that He never shouted. When He created the heavens and earth, in Genesis 1, He never shouted for His creation had no ears to hear. The Pharisees declared that *He spoke with authority not as the scribes,* Matt.7:29; Mk.1:22. Authority is power, when we pray or Speak God's word, we speak with power and authority. When we speak our own words we speak as a mere scribe.

Here again we speak God's word believing in faith and not merely reciting the Word. Therein is the power and authority. I've prayed for some who give verbal affirmation that they believe but their spirit says otherwise. Once again, it can be frustrating for the one interceding.

Honorable Mention

Germaine Copeland has masterfully authored *Prayers that Avail Much,* in three volumes, by Harrison House publishers, which includes numerous categories of prayer with well over a thousand prayers to be prayed in literally every situation known to mankind. I highly recommend her writings. It would be futile for me to attempt to duplicate her works.

For the Word of God is quick and powerful, and sharper than any two edged sword, piercing even to the dividing asunder of soul and spirit, and of the joints and marrow, and is a discerner of the thoughts and intents of the heart. Heb.4:12

Chapter 12

Healing Scriptures

As I ponder these passages I'm reminded that although they were primarily meant for ancient Israel, yet many are meant for the contemporary church. Note: Romans 15:4 *For whatsoever things were written aforetime were written for our learning, that we through patience and comfort of the Scriptures might have hope.* This simply means that whether or not passages apply only to Israel we can still have hope in their message. It also occurred to me of how much I've taken for granted.

Also that many times a passage will "jump out at you" as a direct word from the Lord concerning you as a person, a sort of confirmation of and what He about to do for you. Take these words to heart! Make sure you check the context to be sure you're not taking something out of context to meet your own preconceived thoughts or ideals many have erred in this manner in attempting to prove a point.

These passages are but a few for Scripture is replete with words of healing

Exodus 15:26. *And said, If thou wilt diligently hearken to the voice of the LORD thy God, and wilt do that which is right in his sight, and wilt give ear to his commandments, and keep all his statutes, I will put none of these diseases upon thee, which I have brought upon the Egyptians: for I am the LORD that healeth thee.* Obey God's word and God won't smite you with disease. **See Deuteronomy 27-28.**

Exodus 23:25 *And ye shall serve the LORD your God, and he shall bless thy bread, and thy water; and I will take sickness away from the midst of thee.* Serve the Lord and healing will be yours.

Deuteronomy 7:15 *and the Lord will take away from thee all sickness and will put none of the evil diseases of Egypt, which thou knowest, upon thee; but will lay but will lay them upon all them that hate thee.* God's promise to Israel of evil diseases won't be put on them.

Deuteronomy 28:1-2 *And it shall come to pass, if thou shalt hearken diligently unto the voice of the LORD thy God, to observe and to do all his commandments which I command thee this day, that the LORD thy God will set thee on high above all nations of the earth:*

[2] *And all these blessings shall come on thee, and overtake thee, if thou shalt hearken unto the voice of the LORD thy God.* Obedience brings the blessings.

Deuteronomy 30:19.[19] *I call heaven and earth to record this day against you, that I have set before you life and death, blessing and cursing: therefore choose life, that both thou and thy seed may live:*

[20] *That thou mayest love the LORD thy God, and that thou mayest obey his voice, and that thou mayest cleave unto him: for he is thy life, and the length of thy days: that thou mayest dwell*

in the land which the LORD sware unto thy fathers, to Abraham, to Isaac, and to Jacob, to give them. Choose life.

God's word will not fail to accomplish its purpose

Joshua 21:45 *There failed not ought of any good thing which the LORD had spoken unto the house of Israel; all came to pass.* God's word does not fail.

1Kings 8:56 *Blessed be the LORD, that hath given rest unto his people Israel, according to all that he promised: there hath not failed one word of all his good promise, which he promised by the hand of Moses his servant.*

Psalm 89:34 *My covenant will I not break, nor alter the thing that is gone out of my lips*.

Jeremiah 1:12 *Then the Lord said unto me, Thou hast well seen: for I will hasten my word to perform it.*

Long Life and Healing Promised

2Kings 20:5 *Turn again, and tell Hezekiah the captain of my people, Thus saith the Lord, I have heard thy prayer, I have seen thy tears: behold I will heal thee: on the third day thou shalt go up unto the house of the Lord.*

Psalm 91:16 *With long life will I satisfy him, and shew him my salvation.*

Psalm 103:1-5 *Bless the LORD, O my soul: and all that is within me, bless his holy name.*

2 *Bless the LORD, O my soul, and forget not all his benefits:*

3 *Who forgiveth all thine iniquities; who healeth all thy diseases;*

4 *Who redeemeth thy life from destruction; who crowneth thee with lovingkindness and tender mercies;*

5 *Who satisfieth thy mouth with good things; so that thy youth is renewed like the eagle's.*

Psalm 105:37 *He brought them forth also with silver and gold: and there was not one feeble person among their tribes.* This speaks of Israel's exodus from Egypt.

Psalm 107:20 *He sent His word and healed them, and delivered them from their destructions.* God healed Israel and delivered them, He'll do the same for you and me.

Psalm 118:17 *I shall not die but live, and declare the works of the Lord.* God wants you to live.

Proverbs 4:20-22 *My son, attend to my words; incline thine ear unto my sayings.*

21 *Let them not depart from thine eyes; keep them in the midst of thine heart.*

22 *For they are life unto those that find them, and health to all their flesh.*

23 *Keep thy heart with all diligence; for out of it are the issues of life.*

24 *Put away from thee a froward mouth, and perverse lips put far from thee.* The word of God will save your life

Isaiah 27:5 *or let Him take hold of my strength, that He may make peace with me: and He shall make peace with me.*

Isaiah 41:10-13 *Fear thou not; for I am with thee; for I am thy God: I will strengthen thee; yea I will help thee; yea, I will uphold thee with the right hand of my righteousness.*

[11]*behold, all they that were incensed against thee shall be ashamed and confounded: they shall be as nothing: they that strive with thee shall perish.*

[12]*Thou shalt seek them, and thou shalt not find them, even them that contended with thee: they shall be as nothing, and as a thing of nought,*

[13]*For I the Lord thy God will hold thy right hand, saying unto thee, Fear not; I will help thee.*

Isaiah 43:25-26 *I, even I am He that blotteth out thy transgressions for mine own sake, and will not remember thy sins.*
[26]*Put me in remembrance: let us plead together: declare thou, that thou mayest be justified.* Plead your case to God.

Isaiah 53:4-5 *Surely He hath borne our griefs, and carried our sorrows: yet we did esteem Him stricken, smitten of God, and afflicted.*

[5]*But He was wounded for our transgressions, He was bruised for our iniquities: the chastisement of our peace was upon Him; and with His stripes we are healed.* Jesus bore your/my sins and your sicknesses.

Jeremiah 1:12 *Then the Lord said unto me, Thou hast well seen: for I will hasten my word to perform it.*

Jeremiah 30:17 *For I will restore health unto thee, and I will heal thee of thy wounds, saith the Lord; because they called thee an Outcast, saying, This is Zion, whom no man seeketh after.* God will restore your health.

Hosea 4:6 *Come and let us return unto the Lord: for He hath torn us. And he will heal us; he hath smitten, and he will bind us up.*

Joel 3:10 *Beat down your plowshares into swords, and your pruning hooks into spears: let the weak say I am strong.* You can find strength in God and His word.

Nahum 1:9 *What do ye imagine against the Lord? He will make an utter end: affliction shall not rise up the second time.* Your sickness will leave and not come back again.

Malachi 3:10 *Bring ye all the tithes into the storehouse, that there may be meat in mine house, and prove now herewith, saith the Lord of hosts, if I will not open you the windows of heaven, and pour you out a blessing, that there shalt not be room enough to receive it.* Obey all God's commandments and receive His blessings.

Matthew 8:2-3 *And, behold, there came a leper and worshipped Him saying, Lord, if thou wilt, thou canst make me clean.*
[2] *And Jesus put forth His hand, and touched him, saying, I will; be thou clean. And immediately his leprosy was cleansed.* It is God's will for you to be healed.

Matthew 8: 17 *That it might be fulfilled which was spoken by the prophet Esaias* [Isaiah] *the prophet, saying, Himself took our infirmities, and bare our sicknesses.*

Matthew 18:18-19 *Verily I say unto you, That whatsoever ye shall bind on earth shall be bound in heaven: and whatsoever ye shall loose on earth shall be loosed in heaven.* You can take authority over sickness in your body.

[19] *Again I say unto you, That is two of you shall agree on earth as touching anything that they shall ask, it shall be done for them of my Father which is in heaven.* Agree with someone for your healing.

Matthew 21:21-22. *Jesus answered and said unto them, Verily I say unto you, If ye have faith and doubt not, ye shall only do this which is done to the fig tree, but also if ye shall say unto this mountain, Be thou removed, and be thou cast into the sea; it shall be done.*
[22] *And all these things, whatsoever ye shall ask in prayer, believing, ye shall receive.* Asking in faith and receiving.

Mark 11:22-26 *Jesus answering saith unto them, Have faith in God.*
[23] *For verily I say unto you, That whosoever shall say unto this mountain, Be thou removed, and be thou cast into the sea; and shall not doubt in his heart, but believeth that those things which he saith shall come to pass; he shall have whatsoever he saith.* What you say will make a difference,.
[24] *Therefore I say unto you, What things soever ye desire, ye pray, believe that ye receive them, and ye shall have them.* Believe and you will receive
[25] *And when ye stand praying, forgive, if ye have ought against any: that your Father also which is in heaven may forgive you your trespasses.*
[26] *But if ye do not forgive, neither will your Father which is in heaven forgive your trespasses*

Mark 16:17-18*And these signs shall follow them that believe; In my name shall they cast out devils; they shall speak with new tongues;*

[18] *They shall take up serpents; and if they drink any deadly thing, it shall not hurt them; they shall lay hands on the sick,*

and they shall recover. Have someone lay hands on you for healing.

Luke 10:19-20 *Behold, I give unto you to tread on serpents and scorpions, and over all the power of the enemy: and nothing shall by any means hurt you.*

[20] *Notwithstanding in this rejoice not, that the spirits are subject unto you; but rather rejoice, because your names are written in heaven.* David rejoiced when he cut off Goliath's head! So also should we rejoice in victory!

John 9:31 *Now we know that God heareth not sinners: but if any man be a worshipper of God, and doeth His will, him He heareth.* (Isaiah 1:15; 59:1-2) Worship God;

John10:10 *The thief cometh not, but to steal, kill, and destroy: I am come that they might have life, and that they might have it more abundantly.* The devil wants to kill you, God wants to heal you.

Romans 4:19-22*And not being weak in faith, he considered not his own body now dead when he was about an hundred years old, neither yet the deadness of Sarah's womb:*
[20] *He staggered not at the promise of God through unbelief; but was strong in faith, giving glory to God.*
[21] *And being fully persuaded that, what He had promised, He was also able to perform.*
[22] *And therefore it was imputed to him for righteousness.*
Abraham's unswerving faith in God to provide the promise of Isaac.

Romans 8:11 *But the Spirit of Him that raised up Jesus from the dead dwell in you, He that raised up Christ from the dead shall also quicken your mortal bodies by His Spirit that dwelleth in you.* The Spirit of life is making your body alive.

2Corinthians 10:3-6 *For though we walk in the flesh, we do not war after the flesh:*
4 *(For the weapons of our warfare and not carnal, but mighty through God to the pulling down of strongholds;)*
5 *Casting down imaginations, and everything that exalteth itself against the knowledge of God, and bringing into captivity every thought to the obedience of Christ;*
6 *And having in a readiness to revenge all disobedience when your obedience is fulfilled.* <u>The promise is God will revenge all disobedience when we fulfill our obedience. Too often we want God to move when we are obstinate in not obeying our part.</u>

Galatians 3; 13-14 *Christ hath redeemed us from the curse of the law, being made a curse for us: for it is written, Cursed is every one that hangeth on a tree.*
14 *That the blessing of Abraham might come upon the Gentiles through Jesus Christ; that we might receive the promise of the Spirit through faith.* You are redeemed from the curse.

Ephesians 6:10-18 *Finally, my brethren, be strong in the Lord, and n the power of His might.*
11 *Put on the whole armour of God, that ye may be able to stand against the wiles of the devil.*
12 *For we wrestle not against flesh and blood, but against principalities, against powers, against the rulers of the darkness of this world, against spiritual wickedness in high places.*
13 *Wherefore take unto you the whole armour of God, that ye may be able to withstand in the evil day, and having done all,*
14 *Stand therefore, having your loins gird about with truth, and having on the breastplate of righteousness;*
15 *And your feet shod with the preparation of the gospel of peace;*
16 *Above all, taking the shield of faith, wherewith ye are able to quench all the fiery darts of the wicked.*

[17] *And take the helmet of salvation, and the sword of the Spirit, which is the Word of God;*
[18] *Praying always with all prayer and supplication in the Spirit, and watching thereunto with all perseverance and supplication for all saints.* This truly sums up *Goliath Slaying,* but I wonder how many of us are trained to use God's armour to its fullest? Be strong in the Lord's power. Put on his armour to fight for your healing.

Philippians 2:13 *For it is God which worketh in you both to will and to do of His good measure* God's will, not ours, healing is working in you.

2Timothy 1:7 *For God hath not given us the spirit of fear; but of power, and of love, and of a sound mind.* Fear is not of God.

Hebrews 4:12 For the Word of God is quick, and powerful, and sharper than any two edged sword, piercing even to the dividing asunder of the soul and spirit, and of the joints and marrow, and is a discerner of the thoughts and intents of the heart.

Hebrews 10:23, 25, 35 *Let us hold fast the profesion of our faith without wavering; (for He is faithful that promised.)* You will not waver in your faith [or heart]

[25] *Not forsaking the assembling of ourselves together, as the manner of some is; but exhorting one another: and so much more, as ye see the day approaching.*

[35] *Cast not away therefore your confidence, which hath great recompense of reward.* You can have confidence in God and His word;

Hebrews 11:11*Throu faith Sarah received strength to conceive seed, and was delivered of a child when she was past age, because she judged Him faithful who had promised.*

Hebrews 13:8 *Jesus Christ the same yesterday, today, and forever.* Jesus Christ has never changed. What He did in the Bible He will do for you today.

James 1:5 *If any of you lack wisdom, let him ask of God, that giveth to all men liberally, and upbraideth not: and it shall be given him.* Seek wisdom.

James 3:17-18 *But the wisdom form above is first pure, then peaceable, gentle, and easy to be entreated, full of mercy and good fruits, without partiality, without hypocrisy*
[18] *And the fruit of righteousness is sown in peace of them that make peace.*

James 4:7-8 *Submit yourselves therefore to God. Resist the devil and he will flee from you.*

James 5:14-15 *Is any sick among you? let him call for the elders of the church; and let them pray over him, anointing him with oil in the name of the Lord.*
[15] *And the prayer of faith shall save the sick, and the Lord shall raise him up; and if he hath committed sins, they shall be forgiven him.*
[16] *Confess your faults one to another, and pray one for another, that ye may be healed. The effectual and fervent prayer of a righteous man availeth much.* Be anointed with oil be a Christian who believes in healing [unbelieving Christians are powerless].

1Peter 2:24 *Who His own self bare our sins in His own body on the tree, that we, being dead to sins, should live unto righteousness: by whose stripes ye were healed.* Jesus has already paid the price for your healing.

1Peter 5:7-9 *Casting all your care upon Him; for He careth for you.*
[8] *Be sober, be vigilant; because your adversary, the devil, as a roaring lion, walketh about, seeking whom he may devour.*
[9] *Whom resist steadfast in the faith, knowing that the same afflictions are accomplished in your brethren that are in the world.*

.1John 3:21-22 *Beloved, if our heart condemn us not, then we have confidence toward God.*
[22] *And whatsoever we ask, we receive of Him, because we keep His commandments, and do those things that are pleasing in His sight.* God answers the prayers of those who keep His commandments;

1John 5:14-15 *And this is the confidence that we have in Him, that id we ask any thing according to His will, He heareth us.*
[15] *And if we know He hears us, whatsoever we ask, we know that we have the petitions we desired of Him.* Be confident in your prayers.

3John 2 Beloved, I wish above all things that ye may prosper and be in health, even as thy soul prospereth. Highest wish is for you to be well.

Revelation 12:11 *And they overcame by the blood of the Lamb, and the word of their testimony; and they loved not their lives unto the death.* Give testimony of your healing.

Emotional Healing

Proverbs 2:1-2 *My son, if thou wilt receive my words, and hide my commandments with thee;*
[2]*So that thou incline thine ear to wisdom, and apply thine heart to understanding;* [3]*Yea, if thou criest after knowledge, and lifteth up thy voice for understanding;*
[4] *If thou sleekest her as silver, and searchest for her as hidden treasures*
[5] *Then shalt thou understand the fear of the Lord, and find the knowledge of God.*

Proverbs 4:5-9 *Get wisdom, get understanding: forget it not; neither decline from the words of my mouth.*
[6] *Forsake her not, and she shall preserve thee: love her and she shall keep thee.*
[7] *Wisdom is the principal thing; therefore get wisdom: and with all thy getting understanding.*
[8] *Exalt her and she shall promote thee; she shall bring thee honour, when thou doest embrace her.*
[9] *She shall give to thine head an ornament of grace: a crown of glory shall she deliver to thee.*
[11] *I have taught thee in the way of wisdom; I have led thee in right paths.*
[12] *When thou goes, thy steps shall not be straightened; and when thou runnest, thou shalt not stumble.*
[13] *Take fast hold of instruction; let her not go: keep her; for she* is thy life.

Proverbs 4:25-26 *Let thine eyes look right on, let thine eyelids look straight before thee.*
[26] *Ponder the path of thy feet, and let all thy ways be established.*
[27] *Turn not to the right hand not to the left: remove thy foot from evil.*

1Corinthians 1:30 *But of Him are ye in Christ Jesus, whom God hath made unto us wisdom, and righteousness, and sanctification, and redemption.*

2Corinthians 5:21 *For He hath made Him to be sin for us, who knew no sin; that we might made the righteousness of God in Him.*

Colossians 1:9 *For this cause we also, since the day we heard it, do not cease to pray for you, and desire that ye may be filled with the knowledge of His will in all wisdom and spiritual understanding;*

Colossians 2:3 *In whom are hid all the treasures of wisdom and knowledge.*

James 1:5-8 *If any of you lack wisdom, let him ask of God, ho giveth to al man liberally, and upbraideth not; and it shall be given him.*
6 *But let him ask in faith, nothing wavering. for he that wavereth is like a wave of the sea driven with the wind and tossed.*
7 *For let not that man think he shall receive any thing of the Lord.*
8 *A doubled minded man is unstable in all his ways.*

Health and healing

John 1:14 *And the Word was made flesh, and dwelt among us, (and we beheld His glory, the glory as of the only begotten of the Father) full of grace and truth.*

Romans 8:11*But if the Spirit of Him who raised up Jesus from the dead dwell in you, He that raised up Christ from the dead shall also quicken your mortal bodies by His Spirit that dwelleth in you.*

1Corinthians 6:19-20 *Know ye not that your body is the temple of the Holy Ghost which is in you, which ye have of God, and ye are not your own?*

James 5:13-18 *is there any afflicted among you? let him pray. is any merry? Let him sing psalms.*
[14]*Is any sick among you? Let him call for the elders of the church; and let them pray over him, anointing him with oil in the name of the Lord:*
[15]*And the prayer of faith shall save the sick, and if he have committed sins, they shall be forgiven him.*
[16] *Confess your faults one to another, and pray for one another, that ye may be healed. The effectual fervent prayer availeth much.*
[17] *Elias was a man subject to like passions as we are, and he prayed earnestly hat it might not rain: and it rained not on the earth by the space of three years and six months.*
[18] *And he prayed again, and the heaven gave rain, and the earth gave forth her fruit.*

1Peter 2:24 *Who his own self bare our sine in His own body on the tree, that we, being dead to sins, should live unto righteousness: by whose stripes y were healed.*

3John 2 *Beloved, I wish above all things that thou mayest prosper and be in health, even as thy soul prospereth.*

Psalm 103:3-5 *Who forgiveth all thins iniquities; who healeth all thy diseases;*
[4] *Who redeemeth thy life from destruction; who crowneth thee with loving kindness and tender mercies;*
[5] *Who satisfieth thy mouth with good things; so thy youth is renewed like the eagle's.*

Psalm 107:20 *He sent His word and healed them, and delivered them from heir destructions.*

Proverbs 4:21-22 *Let them not depart from thins eyes; keep them in the midst of thine heart.*
22 *For they are life unto those who find them, and health to all their flesh.*

Isaiah 53:4-5 *Surely he hath borne our griefs, and carried our sorrows: yet we did esteem him stricken, smitten of God, and afflicted.*
5 *But he was wounded for our transgressions, he was bruised for out iniquities: the chastisement of our peace was upon him; and with his stripes we are healed.*

Chronic fatigue

Psalm 3:3-5 *But thou, O Lord, art a shield for me; my glory, and the lifter up of mine head.*
4 *I cried unto the Lord with my voice, and He heard me out of His holy hill. Selah.*
5 *I laid me down and slept; I awaked; for the Lord sustained me.*
6 *I will not be afraid of ten thousands of people, that have set themselves against me round about.*
7 *Arise, O Lord; save me, O my God: for thou hast smitten all mine enemies upon the cheek bone; thou hast broken the teeth of the ungodly.*
8 *Salvation belongeth unto the Lord: the blessing is upon thy people. Selah.*

Psalm 27:1*The Lord is my light and my salvation; whom shall I fear? The Lord is the strength of my life; of whom shall I be afraid?*

Isaiah 51:4 *Hearken unto me, my people; and give ear unto me, O my nation; for a law shall proceed from me, and I will make my judgment to rest for a light of the people.*

Isaiah 61:3*To appoint unto them that mourn in Zion, to give unto them beauty for ashes, the oil of joy for mourning, the garment of praise for the spirit of heaviness; that they might be called trees of righteousness, the planting of the Lord, that He might be glorified.*

Jeremiah 1:12 *Then said the Lord unto me, I will hasten my word to perform it.*

Acts 20:28 *Take heed therefore unto yourselves, and to all the flock, over which the Holy Ghost hath made you overseers, to feed the church of God, which he hath purchased with his own blood.*

Romans 8:2, 10, 11 *For the law of the Spirit of life in Christ Jesus hath made me free from the law of sin and death.*
[10] *And if Christ be in you, the body is dead because of sin; but the Spirit is life because of righteousness.*
[11] *But if the Spirit of Him that raised up Jesus from the dead dwell in you, he that raised up Christ from the dead shall also quicken your mortal bodies by his Spirit that dwelleth in you.*

Galatians 3:13-14 *Christ hath redeemed us from the curse of the law, being made a curse for us: for it is written, Cursed is everyone who hangeth upon a tree.*
[14] *That the blessing of Abraham might come upon the Gentiles through Jesus Christ; that we might receive the promise of the Spirit through faith.*

Ephesians 1:3 *Blessed be the God and Father of our Lord Jesus Christ, who hath blessed us with all spiritual blessings in heavenly places in Christ.*

Ephesians 6:11-13 *Put on the whole armour of God, that ye may be able to stand against the wiles of the devil.*

[12]*For we wrestle not against flesh and blood, but against principalities, against powers, against the rulers of darkness of this world, against spiritual wickedness in high places.*
[13] *Wherefore take unto you the whole armour of God that ye may be able to stand in the evil day, and having all, to stand*

Colossians 1:29 *Whereunto I also labour according to his working, which worketh in me mightly.*

Philippians 4:13 *I can do all things through Christ who strengthens me.*

Hebrews 4:15-16 *For we have not an high priest which cannot be touched with the feelings of our infirmities; but was in all points tempted like as we are, yet without sin.*
[16] *Let us therefore come boldly unto the throne of grace that we may obtain, mercy, and grace to help in time of need.*

1Peter 2:24 *Who his own self bare our sine in his own body on the tree, that we, being dead to sins, should live unto righteousness: by whose stripes ye were healed.*

Persevering with peace

Psalm 3:1-8 *Lord, how are they increased that trouble me? Many are they that rise up against me.*
[2]*Many there be which say of my soul, There is no help for him in God. Selah.*
[3]*But thou, O Lord, art a shield for me; my glory, and the lifter up of mine head.*
[4]*i cried unto the Lord with my voice, and He heard me out of His holy hill.*
[5]*I laid me down and slept; I awaked; for the Lord sustained me.*
[6]*i will not be afraid of ten thousands of people that have set themselves against me round about.*

[7]*Arise, O Lord; save me, O my God: for thou hast smitten all mine enemies upon the cheek bone; thou hast broken the teeth of the ungodly.*
[8]*Salvation belongeth unto the Lord: the blessing is upon thy people. Selah.*

Psalm 66:16-20 *Come and hear, all ye that fear God, and I will declare what He hath done for my soul.*
[17]*I cried unto Him with my mouth, and He was extolled with my tongue.*
[18]*If I regard iniquity in my heart, the Lord will not hear me:*
[19]*But verily God hath heard me; He attended to the voice of my prayer.*
[20]*Blessed be God, which hath not turned away my prayer, nor His mercy from me.*

For my thoughts are not my thoughts, neither are your ways my ways, saith the Lord.[9] For as the heavens are higher than the earth, so are my ways higher than your ways, and my thoughts than my thoughts.[10] For as the rain cometh down, and the snow from heaven, and returneth not thither, but watereth the earth, and maketh it bring forth and bud, that is may give seed to the sower, and bread to the eater:[11] So also shall my Word that goeth forth out of my mouth: it shall not return unto me void, but it shall accomplish that which I please, and it shall prosper in the thing whereto I sent it. Isa.55:8-11.

Topical Index

Chapter 1 Understanding Prayer

Chapter 2 anointing Oil

Chapter 8 Laying on of hands

Chapter 9 Hearing God's Voice

Chapter 10 Compassion

Chapter 11Pray the Word

Chapter 12 Healing Scriptures

What we let into our minds shapes the state of our souls to eventually become giants in our lives. They are called 'home grown' giants.

Bibliography Resources

A Funeral Manual by Perry H. Biddle Jr.

A Hospital Visitation Manual by Perry H. Biddle Jr.

A Marriage Manual by Perry H, Biddle Jr.

Authorized King James Version Bible

Chaplaincy in Law Enforcement by David W, DeRevere; Wilbert A. Cunningham; Tommy W. Mobley, John A. Price

Comparative Study Bible NIV; Amplified; KJV; NASB

Cops by Mark Baker

Crisis Counseling by Scott Floyd

Crisis Pastoral Care by Thomas W. Shane, D. Div.

Crossroads of Life by Richard Godfrey

Manners and Customs of the Bible by James H. Freeman

Healed of Cancer by Dodie Osteen

Our Daily Bread by Radio Bible Class

Pastoral Care for the Aged by Neville A. Kirkwood

Prayers that Avail Much by Germaine Copeland

Praying with Jesus by James Banks

Strongman's His Name…What's His Game by Carol & Jerry Robeson

The Complete Guide to Crisis & Trauma Counseling by Dr. H. Norman Wright

The Eerdmans Bible Dictionary by William B. Eerdmans

The Making of a Cop by Harvey Rachlin

The Tabernacle by Henry, W. Soltau

Understanding the Christian Birthright by Richard Godfrey

When Lightning Strikes A study of Grief by Richard Godfrey

Author's Bookshelf

Crossroads of Life Making Tough Decisions Using Biblical Principles 2011 ISBN 978-4497-2460-3 WestBow Press, Amazon Books

When Lightning Strikes A Time to Mourn a Time to Heal A Study of Grief 2014 ISBN 978-149-4364-786 Amazon Books

Understanding the Christian Birthright A Divinely Inspired, Intricately woven and beautiful Tapestry of the Old and New Testaments 2017 ISBN 978-1511-778-060 Amazon Books

Goliath Slayers A Handbook for Prayer Warriors 2018
ISBN- 13-978-19834-80461
ISBN-10-198-348-0460 Amazon books

Boundaries God's boundaries bring protection, success and prosperity ISBN 978-79406-660 Amazon Books

End Times Study & Satan's Last Stand A Commentary peering into the future & the Ultimate War of Lucifer/Satan against Israel, the Church and Almighty God ISBN 13-978-1725738-578 ISBN-10: 1725728575 Amazon Books

All books may be ordered online through any bookstore or library.

Made in the USA
Monee, IL
10 September 2023